AFGHANISTAN AND THE AFGHANS

BEING A

BRIEF REVIEW OF THE HISTORY OF THE COUNTRY, AND ACCOUNT, OF ITS PEOPLE,

WITH A

SPECIAL REFERENCE

AFGHANISTAN AND THE AFGHANS

BEING A

BRIEF REVIEW OF THE HISTORY OF THE COUNTRY, AND ACCOUNT, OF ITS PEOPLE,

WITH A

SPECIAL REFERENCE

TO

THE PRESENT CRISIS AND WAR WITH THE AMIR SHER ALI KHAN.

BY

H. W. BELLEW, C.S.I.

Author of "Journal of a Mission to Kandahar in 1857-8;" "The Indus to the Tigris;" "Kashmir and Kashghar;" "Dictionary and Grammar of the Paushtoo Language;" "History of the Yosufzuis," &c.

GYAN

Published by

GYAN

Gyan Publishing House
5, Ansari Road
Daryaganj, New Delhi-110002
Phone: 011-47034999, 9811692060
E-mail: books@gyanbooks.com

Distribution Network
gyanbooks.com
India, USA, Canada, UK, Australia, France

ISBN : 978-81-212-2174-0 (HB)
First Published, 1879

2nd Impression 2021

Printed at: Gyan Press, Delhi.

Afghanistan and the Afghans
Being A
Brief Review of the History of the Country, and Account of its people, with a Special Reference
Author: H. W. Bellew

Afghanistan and the Afghans:

BEING A

BRIEF REVIEW OF THE HISTORY OF THE COUNTRY,
AND ACCOUNT OF ITS PEOPLE,

WITH A

SPECIAL REFERENCE

TO

THE PRESENT CRISIS AND WAR WITH THE
AMIR SHER ALI KHAN.

By H. W. BELLEW, C.S.I.

Author of "Journal of a Mission to Kandahar in 1857-8;" "The Indus to the Tigris;" "Kashmir and Kashghar;" "Dictionary and Grammar of the Pushtoo Language;" "History of the Yusufzais," &c.

London:
SAMPSON LOW, MARSTON, SEARLE, & RIVINGTON,
CROWN BUILDINGS, 188, FLEET STREET.
1879.

PREFACE.

The final rupture between our Government and the Amir of Kabul, which has been impending at any time during the past four or five years—and which assumed a more threatening aspect after his contemptuous treatment of the Viceroy's polite invitation to the Imperial Assemblage at Delhi, by which act he signalized himself as the only independent ruler in diplomatic relations with the Government of India who refused to be represented at that august ceremony—has all of a sudden been brought prominently before the British people by the warlike action of Government to resent the premeditated and unprovoked insult of a spoiled and petted barbarian neighbour who has mistaken conciliation for fear, and forbearance for weakness. And the circumstance has naturally led to the public discussion of the causes which have brought about this crisis in the relations heretofore subsisting between that Ruler and ourselves.

In the course of this discussion, as it is represented in the periodicals of the day by the utterances of those who are the guides of public opinion at home, one sees the subject treated piecemeal from different points of view, based upon an isolated occurrence, according to the information and bias of the author or speaker, but nowhere with a comprehensive grasp of the whole case; thus leaving the people to form their opinions upon incomplete premises.

Convinced as I am of the very great importance to our national interests of the thorough comprehension by the nation of the character of our previous relations, and of the nature of our final rupture with the Amir of Kabul, and assured as I am of our power to safeguard our own rights over the whole country which we have assisted him to hold as the frontier province of our own Empire in India, I have ventured to put together for submission to the consideration and inquiry of the nation a very brief account of the country and people ruled by the Amir with whom we are now at war.

The account is in the form of a connected summary of the principal events in the history of the country from the time it came into existence as an independent state, to the time of Sher Ali's defiance, and the march of our troops into his territory; and it concludes with a short account of the main divisions of the country and the several races inhabiting it.

I have attempted to show from its past history, and the heterogeneous character of its population, how utterly unable the country is to maintain its independence as a friendly neighbour without our support, especially in face of the aggressive and disturbing policy pursued by Russia in Central Asia. For we must not lose sight of the fact that Russia is more than ever active in this quarter, and, despite the most solemn and reassuring promises made at St. Petersburg, does not for a moment cease from intrigue and aggression at Tashkand.

It is not a trivial occurrence that Russian officers should, by the Amir's order, find a welcome all over the country, and a Russian

Mission be entertained with unwonted distinction and hospitality at the capital for days before we in India became aware of even their intention to enter the country—an act in direct violation of the solemn pledges of the Russian Government to the contrary. And it becomes a decidedly serious occurrence when, with this friendly treatment offered to the stranger, we, the friends and neighbours of the Amir, and the benefactors to his dynasty, should be jealously excluded, and when our Government asks for the reception of its own Mission, the British Envoy should be threatened with violence, and unceremoniously repelled.

I have attempted to show that with Russia on the border—especially since this infringement of her engagements—the time has come when we can no longer trust to the goodwill or good sense of an uncontrolled manager of our frontier province. The time has come when we must face the necessity of taking the management into our own hands, and this we are perfectly able to do—which is the more satisfactory as the task is a duty we owe to ourselves, to India, and to the people of Afghanistan, whom we have too long left to the forced ignorance and grinding oppression of their rulers. If we fail in our duty to ourselves and to Afghanistan, we shall afford Russia the excuse for interference where she has no possible business that is not directly hostile to us—for interference beyond the field of her legitimate operations—and the consequences will be by no means of a satisfactory kind. Whereas if we plainly assert our rights and stick to them, Russia knows what prudence is, and will refrain from giving us cause to retaliate in Turkistan.

I must explain that in committing this little pamphlet to the notice of the public, my object is to offer a brief and connected account of the history of Afghanistan, and the relations of our Government with its rulers, so far as these have from time to time become known to the public in India; whilst the account of the country and people is written from personal observation and inquiry. I have made no attempt to treat the subject in detail, for that would require volumes, and a leisure which I have not at command; but I have endeavoured to put the case clearly and concisely for a general comprehension of the whole, or for special inquiry into any particular point. If my own views on the subject have become apparent in reading "between the lines," I can only say that they are the conclusions forced upon me by a steady observation for twenty-two years on and about the frontier.

H. W. B.

Lahore, December 6th, 1878.

AFGHANISTAN AND THE AFGHANS.

THE crisis which has long been foreseen by those who have had the opportunity of observing the course of Kabul politics during the last ten or twelve years has at last arrived, and we now find ourselves brought face to face with the dangers against which the press in this country has from time to time raised its voice of warning, and that too in no uncertain tone.

The proverbial fickleness and faithlessness of the Afghan—of which our experience on a former occasion was of a very practical kind—have always been held forward by those who knew the people, as a warning against a too-confiding reliance upon them, and how correctly so is now very forcibly illustrated in the hostile attitude openly assumed by the Amir Sher Ali Khan, our erstwhile professed ally and friend—a finale of his dealings with us which was confidently predicted so long ago as 1869 by more than one observer of his character and mode of government.

The present crisis therefore cannot be supposed to have come upon us entirely unawares, whatever the apparent indifference with which we have kept our eyes shut to the very probable and possible dangers that have during the past five or six years threatened to imperil the peace and safety of India through the unfriendly conduct of the Afghan ruler, whoever he might be. And the conduct of our Government in so long delaying action to coerce the Afghan authorities into proper subordination can only be explained by the overweening confidence with which it viewed the security of its position, and the false hope it entertained of the mollifying and salutary influences of a long-suffering patience and conciliatory good-will.

But be this as it may, the fact of the matter is that we are now at open war with our neighbour on the north-west frontier, and the question of most vital importance to the British Empire at this moment is not so much the consideration and discussion of the causes that have led to this final rupture between the Government of India and the Amir of Kabul, as the consideration and determination of the momentous issues of the hostilities in which we are now engaged—of how and where the war which, despite all our efforts to avert it, has been forced upon us, is to end. For on the right determination of these two points rests the peace of India, and the solution of the difficulty of her north-west frontier.

To approach this subject with a fair chance of arriving at a just appreciation of the facts of the case, it will not suffice for us to carry our inquiry back merely to the time of Lord Auckland's famous Simla Manifesto of forty years ago, nor to revive the sorry memories of that Afghan war. We must carry our retrospect farther back than that, and recall to mind who the Afghans are, and what is their history as an independent nation.

Let us leave the Afghans as a people for description farther on, and for the present let us devote our attention to them as a kingdom. It is not very far back that we have to go, and the briefest review will suffice to put the case clearly before the reader. Let us see what it really tells us as matters of history.

During the latter half of the seventeenth century, when the empire of the Mughal in India and that of the Saffavi in Persia were both in a like state of disorder and fast falling to decay, the Afghans made repeated attempts to throw off the yoke of the Mughal, and in the course of their rebellion the western tribes up to Kandahar fell under the rule of the Saffavi. This, however, was only for a brief interval which ended in the Afghans turning the tables upon their new masters, and destroying their dynasty by the invasion of Persia and sack of Ispahan under the Ghilzai leader Mir Vais of Kandahar. This conquest of Persia was made only by the western Afghans, and was as fleeting as it was sudden, for their wholesale butcheries and horrible excesses of every kind raised enemies against them on all sides, and they were soon driven from the country amidst universal execration of the very name they bore.

During the eight or ten years that the western Afghans were busy ravaging the soil of Persia, their eastern tribesmen were chafing under the repressive efforts of the Mughal governors, and were one by one carving out petty independent chiefships for themselves. And it was in this chaotic state of governments—with anarchy rampant in Persia, and rebellion rife in the western provinces of the Mughal empire in India—that Nadir Shah appeared upon the scene as a world-conqueror. A Turkman bandit himself, he overran Persia with his hordes of slave-hunting robbers of the desert with the speed of only the Turkman rider. He chased the Afghan invaders out of every nook and corner of the country, drove back the Russians from their furtive encroachments on the southern provinces of the Caspian, and completed his victory with the crown of Persia on his head.

But this amount of success did not satisfy the whetted ambition of the conqueror, now encouraged to greater achievements by his easy triumph over Persia, and the alluring prospect offered by the timidity and weakness of the Mughal, and he invaded India with a vast army, which, like all others its predecessors bound on a similar errand from that quarter, was largely composed of Afghans—in this instance the rebellious subjects of the Mughal. His sack of the city of Delhi, and massacre of its inhabitants has—as well may be imagined—left a deeper impression upon the minds of the people of India than the accounts of the almost fabulous wealth he bore away as the spoil of his invasion, and the marvellous tales of which live fresh in the memories of the people who immediately benefited by it.

Nadir Shah was assassinated in his camp just as he reached the borders of his native country, and the bulk of his spoil of India fell into the hands of an Afghan general of cavalry, who had joined his standard with a contingent of ten thousand horse at the outset of his Indian campaign.

This fortunate man was Sardar Ahmad Khan, of the Saddozai section of the Abdali tribe of Afghans. At the time of Nadir's assassination he was present in the camp with the rest of the conqueror's court, but a strong detachment of his troops was on escort duty with the treasure-party, marching up some way in rear of the main army; and on the fact of Nadir's death becoming known he slipped away from the camp with a few followers, and immediately betook himself to Kandahar, in the vicinity of which city, and in the midst of his own people, he came upon the convoy with the treasure.

Ahmad Khan appropriated the treasure, and with its vast and varied stores at his disposal had no difficulty in purchasing the good-will and allegiance, not only of his own clansmen, but of all other Afghans, and of the neighbouring Baloch chiefs as well. And this done, he had himself crowned King of the Durrani, with the title Ahmad Shah, Durri Durràn. The ceremony was performed on a prominent rock of one of the low spurs of hill which project on to the plain near the spot where the treasure was taken, and looking down upon the site of the present city of Kandahar, which was shortly after laid out and built up under the name of Ahmad Shahi or Ahmad Shahr.

These events occurred about the year 1747, and from that date commences the history of the Afghan nation as an independent kingdom. The vast wealth so suddenly and so easily acquired by Ahmad Shah was speedily exhausted in the expenses of starting his newly-formed Empire, and the self-made king was soon obliged to look about for the means of replenishing a very leaky treasury which was ever being drained dry by the insatiable demands of an improvident and reckless nobility who knew no restraint in their newly-acquired habits of pomp and extravagance.

In this difficulty, what was more easy, and more suited to the tastes of the nation than the example of the new king's late master? And so it was that during the twenty-six years of his reign Ahmad Shah managed to keep the Durrani empire going by a succession of seven or eight invasions of India which brought wealth to the imperial treasury, and afforded a welcome outlet for the ambition of his restless nobility, whilst at the same time the power and prestige so acquired enabled him to consolidate his authority all over the country from Lahore in the east to Mashhad in the north-west. Towards the close of his active and eventful reign Ahmad Shah became afflicted by a loathsome disease which destroyed the upper part of his face by a horrible corroding ulceration. He retired to his own little native castle at Marúf in the Tobah hills south of Ghazni, and there died in the midst of the simplicity of his early peasant home. His body was brought to Kandahar, and buried in a court adjoining the palace he had built for himself in the city of his own founding. The mausoleum erected over it is the only building of any architectural merit or substantial structure in the whole city.

His eldest son Tymur Shah succeeded to the throne. He was a weak and voluptuous prince, and removed the seat of government from Kandahar to the gay capital of Kabul. Here he held his court, and soon ran through the treasury left by his father in useless pomp and extravagance, and dissipation of all kinds; and with the results to be naturally expected as the consequence of such a reckless course, in which parade and pleasure took the place of the duties of government and protection of the people. Disorder in society and peril on the roads soon spread all over the country, and law, weak at the capital, became a dead letter in the provinces, where everybody interpreted it for himself, and wielded it at the bent of his will. Under such a system of nursing the infant empire quickly sickened, and sank into a hopeless decline, that too plainly foretold its early death.

During the twenty years of Tymur's reign the empire brought together by his father rapidly fell to pieces. The Panjab under the rising power of the Sikhs, Sind under the Talpur, and Balochistan under the Kambarani Khan, one after the other ignored the upstart Durrani empire, whilst the Persian districts of Ghain, Birjand, Tabbas, and Zawah fell back to Persia, at this time, and for the half-century following the death of Nadir, distracted by the contests of the Zand competitors for the sovereignty, and who by their dissensions prepared the way for the Kajar dynasty, the fourth representative of which—Nasruddin Shah—is now the reigning sovereign at Tehran.

With the death of Tymur Shah in 1793, the downfall of the yet unfledged Durrani empire became complete and irretrievable, after an existence of less than half a century. This prince prior to his death had nominated no successor, but he left half a score of sons by nearly as many different mothers to contest the dwindled remains of the proud heritage he had so unworthily received from his father. In short, the wide empire so hastily and violently and imperfectly brought together by Ahmad Shah had by this time shrunk back to the natural geographical limits of the Afghan people, with the exception only of Kashmir, which was still held as an outlying province of the kingdom.

It is a tedious and sickening task to wade through and sift the successive contentions and rivalries, plots and counterplots, attended as they were by ruthless reprisals and horribly savage barbarities, that mark the history of Afghanistan from the time of Tymur's death till the extinction of his dynasty and the rise of the

Barakzais in 1818. It is enough for our purpose merely to pick out and note the most important events of this troublous period of the history of the country, and more especially with reference to their bearing and influence upon its subsequent condition and present status as an independent government.

The first fact to note is the disruption of the native kingdom, which came to pass almost immediately after Tymur's death, for on the occurrence of this event his several sons, who were either jointly or singly in charge of the several provincial governments of the country—that is to say in Kashmir, Peshawar, Derajat, Kandahar, and Herat—each and all set up as independent princes and claimants of the succession to the throne. So little cohesion was there in the family as a dynasty, and so deep-rooted and rancorous were the jealousies and rivalries of a polygamous offspring, that the hopelessness of a combination or peaceable settlement amongst them soon became apparent, and before long paved the way to a transference of the government into other hands.

During the course of the contest and struggle for supremacy in Afghanistan, which during this period filled the country with bloodshed and anarchy, three of the many sons of Tymur came into prominence as active and determined candidates for the contested throne. These were Zaman Shah, the eldest son, who at the outset possessed himself of the throne for a brief period of tenure: Shuja'-ul-Mulk, his full brother, who held Kandahar, and there plotted his schemes to acquire Kabul; and Mahmud, by another mother, who held

Herat as an independent chief, and declared himself rightful sovereign of all Afghanistan.

Zaman Shah, as Tymur had done during the latter years of his reign, made Peshawar his principal residence. Extravagant, cruel, and oppressive himself, he had the further difficulties of his position—an empty treasury, rebellious family, and factious court to contend against. In this dilemma he contemplated the resuscitation of the fast-fading away glory of the Durranis by a resort to the rich treasure-stores of India—the country which had so often proved a fruitful mine of wealth, and wide field of enterprise to his people under the able guidance of Ahmad Shah—and with this object in view set out on a tour of his kingdom to gather together his people.

The rumours of this projected Afghan

invasion of India so alarmed the Court of Directors of the East India Company—whose possessions and rule were at this time advanced up to Delhi, the seat of the expiring Mughal power—that they forthwith despatched a mission to the court of the Kajar, then but newly established in Persia upon the ruins of the Saffavi empire, for the purpose of utilizing the Persian monarch as a counterpoise to the dreaded designs of the Afghan, and Zaman Shah was thus kept at home through fear of the Persian on his western frontier. With this check to the designs with which he began his reign, the troubles of Zaman Shah thickened around him, and were presently brought to a climax by his impolitic execution of Sardar Payandar Khan, a wealthy and powerful chief of the Muhammadzai section of the Barakzai tribe, who, under the title of Wazir Surfaraz Khan, had created a name and influence for himself, second only to that of the king, as prime minister of Tymur, and Ahmad Shah during his last years.

By this act Zaman Shah at once deprived himself of his best guide, and of his own throne. After a reign of four years he was deposed by Mahmud, and at once deprived of his sight; and now began in earnest the family quarrel. Shah Shuja' lost no time in attacking Mahmud, and after a long pursuit all over the country finally captured and cast him into prison (a mild treatment for which Mahmud was indebted to the new Wazir Fatah Khan), and then himself ascended the throne at Kabul, with Peshawar as his favourite residence. He was no more popular than Zaman, and his long absences from the capital gave his enemies their opportunity.

Fatah Khan, the son and successor in office of the murdered Wazir, determined to avenge Zaman's crime upon his full brother, the Shah Shuja', and became the active partisan of Mahmùd, his half-brother, whom in 1809 he released from prison, and set on the throne at Kabul with himself as Wazir; Shuja' now finding the influence of the Barakzais paramount, and the country arrayed against him, fled from Peshawar, and after many wanderings and sufferings, sought refuge with the Sikh Maharaja at Lahore as a suppliant for his favour. But Ranjit Singh, who had already during the anarchy distracting Kabul possessed himself of the Derajat and Peshawar—the Indus provinces of Afghanistan—and was intent on the subjugation of Kashmir also, had no mind to raise the Afghan from his fallen estate. On the contrary, he inveigled the helpless monarch out of his last hope and means of buying assistance, by extorting from him that precious gem which he had thus far guarded with safety through all his perilous adventures and hardships. And the "Kohinùr"—the far-famed diamond which had successively passed from the Mughal to the Turkman, and from him to the Afghan—now rested with the Sikh, preparatory to its transfer to the glorious crown of England, where, let us hope, it is destined to shine with undiminished splendour till the end of time.

After this Shah Shuja', in terror of his life, quitted the inhospitable territory of the Sikh, and in 1815 threw himself on the bounty of the East India Company, who assigned him a pension and a residence at the frontier town of Ludhiana—a town which sprang into existence under the rule of the former Pathan kings of Delhi, and has since been famous as the asylum of the broken-down princes of their native land, whilst, curiously enough, it still affords a secure and peaceful retreat to the sons and descendants of the refugee, who now found rest and shelter within its hospitable walls. We must here leave Shah Shuja' for the present, and revert to the history of events in Kabul.

The events occurring in Afghanistan at this period mark the date when the fate of the country as an independent kingdom was already doomed. In fact the Afghan kingdom had at this time ceased to exist, and it did not recover from its dismemberment so as to become developed into a consolidated state until only the other day, when, at the close of his reign, the Amir Dost Muhammad Khan recovered Herat to the Kabul government.

Shah Mahmùd had not long been on the throne of Kabul, before he awoke to the fact that he was but a mere puppet in the hands of his wily minister, who held all the power in his own keeping, and took care to strengthen his position against assault by distributing the several provincial governments of the country, and other posts of importance, amongst the members of his own family and immediate adherents. The power thus acquired by Fatah Khan aroused the jealousy and suspicion of Kamran, the son and heir of Mahmùd, who saw in the minister a dangerous rival to the throne, and he therefore put him out of the way. Fatah Khan was murdered with shocking barbarity and cruel torture in 1818, and the whole country was again at once convulsed with anarchy.

Mahmùd and Kamran retired to Herat, whilst the rest of the country became divided between the brothers of the murdered Wazir. Kabul, with Jalalabad and Ghazni, fell to Dost Muhammad Khan; Kandahar, with Kalati Ghilzai and Girishk, became the joint possession of the brothers Kohndil, Purdil, and Rahmdil; and Peshawar, with Yusufzai and Kohat, was held by the brothers Pir Muhammad, Sultan Muhammad, and Sayyid Muhammad, as tributaries of the Sikhs, who presently occupied the province with a strong military force; whilst Kashmir and Derajat were also lost to the Sikhs.

Such was the disordered and dismembered state of Afghanistan during the early years of the present century, when we first became acquainted with the country and its people, through the successive missions of Malcolm to Persia and the journey of Elphinstone to Peshawar. If we review the history of Afghanistan during this period—the first quarter of the present century—we shall see how completely the newly-raised power of the Durrani had sunk, never to rise again, or even to maintain a separate existence as an independent government exercising sovereign authority.

At the close of the last, and opening of the present centuries, when Afghanistan was the home of discord and strife amongst the princes of the Saddozai family, Persia had emerged from her anarchy under the

Zand chieftains and become a settled kingdom under the Kajar dynasty. Bukhara was still the sport of Shah Murad—the religious fanatic and political impostor Rahim Bai—whose eccentricities and pious austerities gained him a saintly reputation, and whose ignorance and licence deprived the country of all semblance of law. Balochistan had since some years become a consolidated Khanate under Mihrab Khan, a local chief of the Kambarani family. Sind also had become settled under its Talpùr governors. The Derajat, Peshawar, and Kashmir, not yet taken by the Sikh, were still held by princes of the Saddozai family. And the Panjab had, under the stimulus of a newly developed religion, grown into a compact confederacy of Sikh chieftains, with Ranjit Singh as their head.

Such, in brief terms, was the political situation in and around the Khorassan province of the Mughal emperors, when, in 1809, Elphinstone's mission made its way to Peshawar, and in the following year Malcolm carried his third embassy to the court of Persia. At this time, too, were broached the Franco-Russian designs against the British power in India by Napoleon Bonaparte. So much for the surrounding situation. How it fared in the interior of Afghanistan at and immediately subsequent to this period we have already seen—the downfall of the Saddozai, and the rise of the Barakzai, the transfer of rule from the family of the Durrani Shah to the family of the Durrani Wazir. With the exception of Mahmùd at Herat, where he reigned as an independent sovereign, there were now no representatives of Tymur left in the country. They had all disappeared from the scene, either removed by death, or driven into exile in India.

Amongst the latter was Shah Shuja', and with him thus disposed of, the Barakzais to all appearance had the rule of Afghanistan to themselves. How greatly its extent had become reduced from the empire left by the founder of the independence of the nation only a short half-century before, will have been gathered from the preceding review of the history of the country. At this time, indeed, the usurped authority of the Barakzais was confined to the narrow limits of Kabul and Kandahar only, and in this restricted area Dost Muhammad Khan, as in possession of the capital, exercised the supreme authority, such as it was, under the title of

Amir, or "military commander." And it was to him, as the most prominent personage in the country, that Burnes was sent on a mission of commerce and discovery about the year 1835.

The mission of Burnes to Kabul proved to be the prelude to a new phase in the history of Afghanistan, and marks the era of a complete revolution in the political status of that country as an integral part of that geographical area which in recent times has become so familiarly known as Central Asia—a region the affairs and peoples of the several petty states of which were henceforth destined to emerge from the obscurity that had shrouded them since the middle ages, and to grow in increasing interest to the nations of the world. But this is not all. The opening out of this close-shut region, the petty principalities of which were ever varying in limits, and ever at war amongst themselves, and in which, without exception, the fanatic bigotry and ignorance of an exclusive and intolerant *Islam* racked the land with anarchy and oppression, and enslaved the people in the chains forged by an arrogant and jealous priesthood—the opening out of this region was destined sooner or later, but infallibly, nevertheless, to involve the two Great European Powers, whose might and greatness were inseparably connected with their respective conquests and empire on the broad field of the Asiatic continent in a vigilant and jealous rivalry for the maintenance there of a just equilibrium.

In the determination of this point of balance Russia and England were henceforth destined to work, and that not as a mere matter of choice or ambition, but as the imperious necessity of the birth and growth of their Asiatic empires—a necessity which must by the very nature of the situation yet impel them onwards, each in his sphere, till the natural boundary between the different countries and nations of the north and the south is reached. Until, in fact, the natural geographical and ethnological and political boundary between the Tatar and Aryan races in Asia shall be recognized as the line of demarcation between Russia in Asia and England in Asia.

Where this boundary-line is, and when it will be acknowledged as the fixed line of separation between Russia and England, are questions that are gradually answering themselves by the logic of facts and the onward roll of time. But their investigation and due appreciation by us are all the same matters of the utmost interest and importance from a national point of view. Because the future security, peace, and prosperity of the Empire depend on the proper settlement of this boundary-line.

Before we approach this subject, however, it is necessary to take up the history of Afghanistan again, and to continue our summary review of its most important events up to the present time, in order that we may enter upon the inquiry—and this will gradually unfold itself and be developed when we come to consider who the Afghans are, and what is their country —with a fair knowledge of the facts of the case.

We have already noted that when Burnes took his mission to Kabul, the rule of the recently established Barakzai was restricted within the narrow limits of that province and Kandahar; that the Indus provinces were in the possession of the Sikh; and that Herat only was held by the Saddozai in the person of Mahmùd, who, as such, styled himself Shah or "king," and kept up a small royal court there; whilst Shah Shuja' had settled down quietly in his retreat at Ludhiana to await the next turn in the wheel of his fortune.

And we must now note that the same causes which prompted the British Government in India, with the frontier at the river Sutlaj, to send their emissary into Afghanistan and its surrounding states, also prompted the Russian Government, with its Asiatic frontier at the lower course of the Jaxartes, or Siyr Darya, to send its own emissaries into the same quarters. These causes were the disruption of the Durrani empire of Ahmad

Shah and the redistribution of its outlying provinces in the directions of the growth of the English and Russian conquests from the south and the north respectively.

As a consequence of the reports furnished by their several agents, both governments entered actively into a participation in the political affairs of the different independent states intervening between their own territories, and, naturally, each with objects at variance with the interests of the other. And so it came to pass that Russia, as a counterfoil to the occupation of Peshawar by the Sikh, set the Persian to seize Herat—the Panjab in the east being in much the relative position to the British on the Sutlaj that Persia was to the Russian on the Caspian.

Now Herat as the frontier fortress of the

former Mughal province of Khorassan was always, as it still is, considered to be the gate of India and the key of Afghanistan. And its possession by Persia, or any other power but Afghanistan, of which it formed an integral part, was not to be allowed by the British if they wished for peace or safety in India; for Herat commanded Balkh, which was the Oxus province of the empire of Ahmad Shah, in the north, and Kandahar, which was a home province, in the south.

So the British Government took measures to ensure the independence of Herat, and to revive the extinct Durrani empire, as a buffer against Russian intrigue and Persian encroachment from the west. The idea, there is no doubt, especially in the light of subsequent events, was as correct in its propriety and conception as it was faulty in its details and execution.

The invasion of Afghanistan, the restoration of Shah Shuja' to the throne of Kabul, the release of Herat from the Persians and their Russian coadjutors, and the recognition of Shah Mahmùd and his successor, Shah Kamran, as independent sovereigns at Herat were the first results of our triumphal initiation of the policy forced upon the British Government by the necessities of the time and the occasion. Their quickly following failure, and our own disasters at Kabul, were the very natural results of injudicious interference and divided authority in the one case, and of inexcusable neglect of ordinary military precautions in the other.

Having set the ousted monarch on his throne, we should have left him alone to organize his government in the manner best suited to his people, and of which he was the proper judge, and not have hampered him as we did with fussy political officers, pulling him this way and that, and daily dragging his authority in the dust before the eyes of his own subjects. As for the blunders of our military commanders, whatever palliation may be pleaded on the grounds of their subordination to political authority, there can be no excuse for their neglect of the standard principles of their profession. The disastrous issue of affairs at Kabul, in the light of the brilliant achievements of Sale at Jalalabad, and of Nott at Kandahar, appears the darker blot upon the otherwise bright page of our operations in Afghanistan; and, though fully retrieved by the avenging army under Pollock, has left a stain which has not yet entirely faded from the minds of the Afghans, notwithstanding the facts that we have since that unhappy day advanced our border to the very door of their house, and survived the mutiny with a stronger life than ever.

Our protégé, Shah Shuja', perished in the revolt and massacre at Kabul, and his numerous family became pensioners upon the bounty of the British Government, or were provided for by appointments in the public services, a number of the former constituting quite an Afghan colony in the "Princestown" suburb of Ludhiana. Whilst Dost Muhammad Khan, who with his favourite wife and younger sons was a prisoner of war in India, was released to find his way back to the capital and rule from which we had so unceremoniously and unwisely ousted him on behalf of the Saddozai, for as a Durrani himself he was just as good, and as a popular chief a much better instrument in our hands than the puppet of our choice.

Dost Muhammad returned to Kabul all the wiser for his travels and experiences in India, and fully impressed with the might and resources of the British Government; an impression which time did not diminish, for up to the close of his life his repeated injunctions to his sons were that, whatever might be their future differences with the British, they were never to desert their friendship and alliance. He was welcomed back to his country as the Amir whom the people loved, and he quickly recovered his previous influence and authority within its former limits, Herat remaining independent under Shah Kamran, and Kandahar being held jointly by the brothers Kohndil, Purdil, and Rahmdil.

And so ended our ill-directed attempt to

resuscitate an extinct empire, which in its palmiest days never possessed any cohesion, and which even at this time, under the altered circumstances of its surroundings, had less chance than ever of providing the wherewithal to carry on the government as an independent kingdom. For it must be borne in mind that the origin of the empire was an accident, arising out of the sudden and unexpected acquisition of vast wealth; that the internal resources of the country yielded nothing to the imperial treasury; that the state coffers were replenished from time to time by plundering expeditions into India; and that when this source of supply became closed—as has been shown in the preceding pages—the government collapsed, and the empire fell to pieces.

In fact the country, which as part of a great empire was fully capable of meeting the expenses of its civil and police administration, and of taking its share of the burden of imperial defence, was by itself as an independent state utterly unable to preserve internal order or external security, or even to continue as an integral whole. For its mere existence as an independent state it was, and still is, essentially necessary that it derive support from without, either by conquest or diplomacy; and in the absence of such maintenance, the state must forego its independence and merge into the territory or political system of one or other of its paramount neighbours. The truth of this is very plainly exemplified in the history and experience of Afghanistan ever since the restoration of Dost Muhammad to the government of Kabul.

Had we after our evacuation of the

country in 1842-3 thereafter rigidly abstained from all interest in its affairs, and consistently withheld our support from its rulers, there is, I believe, not the smallest doubt that Afghanistan would have become long ago, if not territorially, at the least politically either Persian or Russian ground. For there is no gainsaying the fact that it has been the repeated occurrence of the impending danger of this very catastrophe which has, during the past quarter of a century, kept our Government on the alert, and drawn from it a very consistent and powerful support, both material and moral —a support which, as will be seen farther on, has, so long as it lasted, been given free of any return, and in consequence yielded no result beyond the mere existence of the country as an independent government, and, thanks to our good offices and friendly recognition, as a now consolidated state in the hands of a single ruler.

But this growth and unification of rule has brought upon the ruler a greater burthen of government, and with of course increased necessities—necessities which could only be met by the home resources through a complete reorganization and remodelling of the system of the internal administration of the country under the protection of its paramount and friendly neighbour. And failing this, the necessities of the ruler would compel him to look abroad for that external support without which his government could not endure, nor his kingdom be saved from dismemberment, or lapse into other hands. Heretofore the sources of revenue dependent on a good administration have not been developed or economized through ignorance and national incapability, whilst the external support hitherto derived freely and gratuitously from the British Government has now ceased through failure of reciprocity and co-operation on the part of a suspicious and ill-disposed ruler. But being necessary all the same under the existing uncontrolled and corrupt government, it will be sought for in other quarters. All this will be more clearly seen and understood as we proceed with our review of the history of the more recent events occurring in Afghanistan.

Following upon our withdrawal from Afghanistan and Balochistan, and our abandonment of them for the time being to their own devices under local chiefs of the native races, came the campaigns in Sind and the Panjab, and the conquest and annexation of both to the British dominion in Asia—a glorious redemption of the Kabul misadventure. The contest was a tough one against worthy foes, and in the case of the latter country against the vigorous nationality of a people who were themselves the growing conquerors of the Afghan.

The conclusion of the Sikh war in 1849 planted the British arms and rule at Shikarpur and the mouth of the Bolan in the one direction, and at Peshawar and the mouth of the Khybar in the other. But in this advance across the Indus—the the eastern boundary of the Khorassan province—to the very threshold of the doors leading into Kabul we took up our position on no pre-arranged plan of conquest, or preconceived limit of frontier. We found ourselves planted across the

Indus at the foot of the Suleman range simply as the inheritors by conquest of the Sikh kingdom—a kingdom which had itself only recently extended in its continuous growth by conquest to this assuredly, but for our intervention, temporary line.

In fact we took up and accepted the frontier the Sikh happened to possess at the time we conquered him, and no more. The merits or the demerits of the line as a defensive frontier were never preconsidered. The line was simply adopted as the heritage of our triumph over its Sikh possessor. And this is the true and the only explanation of our position along a line of frontier so indefensible against external assault, and so weak strategically as a peaceable and secure boundary.

Let us see what this frontier really is. Well, if we consult a good map, we shall find that it is represented by a wavy line, not everywhere well defined, which extends for about eight hundred miles from north to south along the eastern skirts of the Suleman range and its offshoots northward, to the network of mountains which fill the angle of junction between the Himalaya and the Hindu Kush.

Omitting Kashmir territory, which extends down to Chilas, the line commences at the top of the adjoining Kaghan valley, skirts the Black Mountain, below which it crosses the Indus at the foot of the Mahaban, and then circles round the Peshawar Valley as far as the Khybar Pass. Here, without touching the pass itself, it is thrown back towards the Indus, and, passing across the Afridi hills where they meet the Khattah range, reaches Kohat. From this point it projects westward along the base of the Orakzai and Zaimukht hills (the northern boundary of the Miranzai valley) to the Kurram river at Tall. Here it is again deflected along the base of the Waziri hills (the southern boundary of Miranzai), and passing round their eastern spurs to the Bannu district, is continued onwards with lesser ins and outs along the base of the Suleman range, down to the Sind frontier and the Arabian Sea.

The peculiar feature of this frontier-line is its domination by the mountain range, the base of which it skirts. This range of mountains, though forming a continuous chain, presents many irregularities, is indented by a succession of narrow valleys draining to the Indus, and is pierced by a series of passes, several of which are used as trade routes and military roads. The whole range is inhabited by a multitude of wild highlanders, divided into endless clans and tribes, but all ranged under three distinct nationalities, speaking different languages, distinctly of the Indian stock, and they are more or less entirely independent,—they are the Baloch in the south, the Hindki in the north, and the Pathan in the intermediate portion of the range, including the Suleman and Khybar hills. The Pathan tribes upon the western slopes, and in the valleys debouching upon the Indus riverain, are more or less under the control of the Kabul ruler either directly or indirectly, and thus the command of the passes is held on that side.

It is at the foot of such a barrier that our frontier lies. The line here skirts the foot of the hills; there it runs across a bit of open plain; elsewhere it juts into some mountain glen, or runs round the end of some projecting spur. It is in short the line formed by the Sikh tax-gatherer, and included merely those villages which the Sikh arms had in their yet youthful career —nipped in the bud by us—subjugated to the payment of revenue. This frontier nowhere commanded any of the passes debouching upon it, nor did it give its possessors the smallest control or influence over the country beyond.

Had the Sikhs been left in possession of this line of frontier, they could not, I believe, have possibly retained it with safety, peace, or profit. No government but a great, powerful, enlightened, and benevolent one, such as is ours, could have held such a frontier as we have done during the thirty years of our tenure of it; notwithstanding that we have had to carry fully as many military expeditions of a punitive kind more or less far into the hills beyond it. And to this course of retaliation we were compelled, be it remembered, during a period of unbroken peace with the independent states beyond it. So long as peace with these continued, or was assured, the inconvenience of a faulty frontier-line might have been endured as a necessary evil. But in the absence of such assurance of our safety the line becomes untenable, and the instinct of self-preservation renders its rectification an indispensable necessity. What this rectification should be, and where in advance we should take up our final position—for I take it for granted that a retrograde step is out of the question altogether—is the most momentous question that now requires the matured consideration and well-weighed decision of the

British nation. And upon the manner in which they settle it will depend the safety and endurance of the empire. With our frontier neighbour an open enemy, there is no question of the necessity for a rectification of the frontier—a frontier which is pierced in front by a dozen passes, not one of which is in our hands, whilst an unbridged river of the first magnitude and annually flooded for four months, flows in rear,—the question is the nature and extent of this necessary rectification, for so long as he remained our friend and we could rely upon his loyalty, the territory of our neighbour was our real frontier; and on those terms it served our purpose to leave it in his keeping. Those conditions being reversed, a change—the nature of which has to be decided—becomes for us a matter of inevitable necessity.

We cannot too carefully consider this subject, for upon the nature of our treatment of it depend issues of the most vital importance to the safety and prosperity of the empire, not only in the present, but in the future as well. I have said that we took up our line of frontier across the Indus without previous inquiry into its merits or demerits as a boundary-line, or investigation into its capabilities as a defensible position. We merely received it as it was, faulty or not, in virtue of our annexation of Sind, and succession to the dominion of the Sikh; and we have kept it intact, neither receding from it, nor advancing (with the exception of the little valley of Miranzai, which we brought within the frontier-line in 1855) beyond it, simply because we have from the first until now had no cause of hostility with our neighbours on its other side. So long as these neighbours continued our friends and allies, and there was no danger pressing upon their distant frontiers, for so long it was a matter of mere inconvenience, or perhaps indifference, to us whether our actual administrative frontier was on this side of the passes or on that. But the acceptance of this inconvenience, or the endurance of this indifference could obtain only on the evident condition of the assured friendship and loyalty of our neighbours in actual possession of the passes. So soon as this condition ceased to exist, the situation based upon it also ceased to exist, and with this change the whole question of the frontier enters upon a new phase.

Under the Mughal empire so long as Kabul, Kandahar, and Herat were loyal and tributary to India, the security of the passes was assured, and the Delhi emperors were content with this proviso to leave the hill-tribes to their poverty, lawlessness, and independence, as the most economical and peaceable arrangement for the safety and prosperity of the empire. But when any of these distant frontier rulers rebelled or showed signs of defection, the empire at once put forth its might to reduce the recalcitrant to obedience and subjection as a necessity of its own vitality. And so it has been with us, the successors of the Mughal in Northern India. So long as the rulers of the frontier states remained friendly and loyal to us, we were assured of the safety of the passes into our territory which they held. But when they turn from their friendship and loyalty to us, with them goes that safety of our position which rested in their hands, and then arises for us the necessity of securing the safety of our position as a condition of our own vitality. Now let us consider what have been the conditions on which we have heretofore held the frontier taken over from the Sikh and the Sindi rulers. As to the case of the latter we may dispose of it in a few words, because the Khan of Kalàt—the titular ruler of Balochistan, and holder of the Bolan pass—has always proved amenable and sufficiently alive to his own interests to throw in his lot with the British; whilst at the same time the accident of his geographical position has shielded him from the temptations that have beset and exercised his more powerful neighbour of Afghanistan. Besides, his subjects—the Baloch and the Brahoe—are men of very different calibre to the subjects of the Kabul ruler—the Afghan and the Pathan. Accordingly the Sind frontier (administered by the Bombay Government on a system different to and distinct from that which under the Panjab Government obtained on the rest of the line northwards) in the course of a few years became settled—that is to say, settled as much as a frontier-line of this kind could be expected to be so—and, despite internal dissensions and disorders, the ruler of Balochistan received a British officer as Political Resident at his court, and by this public token cemented his alliance with the British Government—an alliance which after many years of experience he renewed and strengthened by his presence and participation in the ceremonies of the Imperial Assemblage held at Delhi in the beginning of last year; and an alliance which he has since confirmed by his practical loyalty in the surrender of Quetta as a military outpost of the suzerain empire.

As to the former, the case is different.

With the annexation of the Panjab we became the rulers of a million of Pathans and Afghans who occupied the Trans-Indus territories of the Sikhs. These people passed under our sway, not by the rights of direct conquest, but as the recently conquered subjects of a defeated foe, and though towards the close of the Sikh war the Amir Dost Muhammad and his then youthful son, the present Amir Sher Ali, came down as far as Attock in the futile attempt to recover Peshawar to the Kabul Government—during the first years of our rule, and indeed up to the time of the Indian Mutiny, considered themselves an unconquered people.

Time, however, and good government have worked wonders in reconciling these compatriots of the Afghan and former fellow-subjects of the Durrani empire to the situation; and they are now, considering the peculiar circumstances of their position, as orderly and industrious a people as are to be found in any other part of the Panjab. Their increase in wealth, prosperity, and domestic security under the British rule is, to use one of their own similes, as "clear as the noonday sun;" and these advantages have not escaped the notice of their fellow-countrymen beyond the frontier-line; nor have they failed to excite in them a desire for participation in the like blessings.

The desire, though suppressed as to expression beyond the border through fear of the authorities there, is none the less strong, and within our limits finds free vent amongst those who come this way to labour or to trade—a party whose aggregate numbers visiting India annually cannot be much less than forty thousand, mostly adult men. It appears in fact, that, with the exception of the ruling classes and government officials, the whole of the settled population of the country—excluding of course the hill-tribes who have always been independent in their mountain retreats—is looking forward to the day of release from the thraldom of their oppressors by the happy advance across the passes of the British rule, and which they are persuaded cannot be long deferred.

This is the sentiment which is now predominant in the minds of the people in the towns and villages of Afghanistan, from what they see and hear of our rule in India. And it was the sentiment which possessed their minds at the time of our withdrawal from their country in 1843, after only three or four years' experience of our rule under military law. But so far as the interests of the native rulers was concerned, this was far too dangerous a sentiment to permit the growth of, or even to allow the existence of. And Dost Muhammad, when he returned to Kabul, took every means in his power to crush out and efface from the minds of his people the good opinion those who had been brought into contact with us formed of us as a nation.

He shut up his country against access from the side of India, and maintained a most vigilant supervision over all his own subjects entering or returning from its territories. He encouraged a fanatic and bigoted priesthood to preach us down as infidels and everything that was vile, till presently the term "Farangi" was used by mothers as a bogy to frighten naughty children into good behaviour. In his own court and official audiences he allowed our name to be vilified and coupled with opprobrious epithets, and to slay the unarmed and unoffending European was considered a meritorious act.

The exclusive and depreciatory policy thus introduced by Dost Muhammad as a means of suppressing the natural bias of his subjects in our favour—a bias which was very largely the result of self-interest as created by the commercial relations of his people with India—was enforced with unabated vigilance on the advance of our position to the mouth of the Khybar; and the same attitude of suspicion and exclusion has been rigidly observed by his successors in the government as the only secure foundation on which the maintenance of their own despotic authority rested.

With the adoption of such a line of policy at the outset of his resumption of the government of Kabul, Dost Muhammad maintained a wary reserve in his relations with the Government of India; and, in fact, for several years there was a complete blank in the diplomatic correspondence between the two governments. The interval, however, was by no means an idle time at Kabul.

The prospect of the enlargement of the Amir's government by the incorporation of the Indus provinces having faded away in the presence of the British garrisons established at Peshawar and the Derajat, Dost Muhammad was content to secure his positions in the Kurram and Daur valleys debouching upon the riverain of Kohat and

Bannu. He next turned his attention to the security of his capital from the north, in which direction he feared the hostility of the Amir of Bukhara, from whom he had received but a shabby shelter as a refugee on the occasion of his flight from Kabul before our invading army in 1839. For this purpose it was essentially necessary that he should hold in his own hands not only the passes themselves of the Hindu Kush, but also the approaches to them on the other side. Accordingly he commenced to set his house in order by recovering to Kabul the northern frontier of the Durrani empire of Ahmad Shah. By the end of 1850 Dost Muhammad had conquered Balkh, and annexed this province of Turkistan to Afghanistan with the Oxus, or "Amu Darya," as boundary down to Khwaja Salih; and the conquest has been maintained unopposed ever since.

Thus secured towards the north, the Dost, as he is familiarly styled by us, entered upon that scheme of consolidation for the rest of Afghanistan under a single ruler, which—owing to the jealousies and personal interests of the local chiefs, which he was unwilling to disturb violently for fear of embroiling his family and country in anarchy and civil war—was only completed at the close of his eventful life by the occupation of Herat in 1863. This project for the consolidation of the Afghan territories beyond our frontier into a united kingdom under a single and undivided authority was, so far as concerned that country itself, the only prospect that offered the means (under a good administration of course) of maintaining the government as an independent and defensible state worthy the alliance and support of its powerful neighbours, whilst at the same time it vastly enhanced the political influence of its sovereign for good or evil towards us.

The scheme, however, was not easily or promptly executed, owing to the jealousies of the local Afghan chiefs in possession at Kandahar and Herat, and the intrigues they fostered with Persia and Russia. It was not till 1854 that the Dost succeeded in establishing his authority at Kandahar as the first step towards the accomplishment of his design; and the occasion gave rise to so fresh a current of intrigue with Persia in the interest of the ousted family of Rahmdil Khan that Dost Muhammad, to strengthen his hands, made overtures to the Government of India for the renewal of friendly relations. His action in this matter was the more acceptable to the British Government, inasmuch as, from their position as the possessors of the eastern provinces of Afghanistan, they were very seriously interested and compromised in the status and fate of the rest of that country. The Amir's overtures were received in a conciliatory spirit by the Government of India, and the result was the conclusion of a treaty of friendship, early in 1855 at Peshawar, between Sir John Lawrence and Sardar Ghulam Hydar Khan, on behalf of the Government of India and the Amir Dost Muhammad Khan respectively.

This Sardar was a younger son of the Amir, and had been nominated heir apparent in succession to his elder brother, the notorious Muhammad Akbar Khan, who figured so prominently in the Kabul rebellion and massacre of 1841. During the British occupation of Afghanistan he and his younger brother, the present Amir Sher Ali Khan, were domiciled in India as prisoners of war. He was not, therefore, an entire stranger to the people he had come to negotiate with on behalf of his father, not to mention his experience of their good offices on his part at the siege and capture of Ghazni, when his life was saved from the vengeance of the Saddozai.

As the first rapprochement between the two governments since the Afghan war this treaty in its three brief articles expressed no more than the establishment of friendship between the two contracting parties, and affairs on the frontier remained much as they were. But at Kandahar intrigues continued rife, and on the death in the following year of Yar Muhammad Khan, the minister and successor of Shah Kamran in the government of Herat, the Persians stepped in and took possession of the place. This infringement of Afghan territory led to the declaration of war against Persia by the British Government, and the conclusion of a treaty of friendship and alliance between the Government of India and the Amir of Kabul, which was signed at Peshawar in January, 1857, by Dost Muhammad Khan in person, and Sir John (now Lord) Lawrence on the part of the Government of India. At the same time it was arranged to despatch a mission of British officers to Kandahar, for the purpose of aiding the Amir with counsel and advice, and organizing an Afghan force for the recapture of Herat from the Persians. Major (now Sir H. B.) Lumsden was selected to command the mission, and at the same time a native agent was appointed to the court of the Amir at Kabul. The Government of India also presented Dost Muhammad with several thousand muskets, and granted him a subsidy of a lakh of rupees a month so long as the war lasted; and the grant was afterwards continued for the eighteen months that the mission remained in Afghanistan.

On this occasion of his visit to Peshawar, Dost Muhammad, notwithstanding the prompt and liberal support accorded to him by the British Government, firmly declined to open his country to British subjects, and positively refused to receive British officers as political residents, on the plea of his inability to protect them against the violence of his turbulent subjects—a plea he might justly advance, considering his own action in keeping alive and fostering their animosity against us. And it was on the grounds of this professed inability to guarantee its safety there, that the mission was sent to Kandahar and not to Kabul, the centre in which the British name was publicly denounced and vilified with the consent and tacit encouragement of the authorities; whilst, as a compromise with the rejected demand for political officers on his frontiers, the Dost consented to receive a Musulman agent at Kabul, à concession which he considered sufficient return for our support of his cause. With the installation of this official at Kabul as the Mission proceeded on its way to Kandahar, diplomatic relations between the Amir and the Government of India were established on a recognized footing.

Lumsden's Mission had hardly arrived at its destination when peace was concluded with Persia, Herat restored to the Afghan, and India plunged in the extremity of peril by the mutiny of the Native Army. The occasion was one of those catastrophes which bring out a nation's might, and show the stuff her men are made of, and India emerged from the death struggle of the Sepoy revolt with a new lease of life in the hands of Great Britain. She has entered upon her new career with a vigour and earnestness of purpose which foretell a bright and great future; and she is now stronger and more loyal than ever to the empire that has made her what she is.

The time of England's sore adversity and trial in India was also a time of trial of a very different kind in Afghanistan, where the British operations centred around Delhi

—the for the moment revived Mughal capital—were watched with the keenest anxiety and interest, in impatient expectation of that favourable opportunity which it was hoped would open the way for action to recover to Kabul at least the Indus provinces, if no more. The treaty concluded by the Amir with the Government of India at the beginning of the year was barely dry on the paper which recorded its terms, when Dost Muhammad was confronted with the urgent question of fidelity to his bond. The temptation to repudiate the contract was severe, and for a while the decision of the Amir wavered in the balance between the claims of loyalty to his compact and the dictates of self-interest. There was a strong party at Kabul urging on the Amir the folly of letting pass so good an opportunity to recover Peshawar without making an attempt to benefit by its promising issues, and prominent amongst its members was Sardar Sher Ali Khan, younger brother of the heir apparent, and now the ruling Amir of Afghanistan. The arguments of this warlike party were telling upon the uncertain mind of the Dost, when Sardar Azim Khan, an elder brother by another mother, put the case so sensibly before the court, that his advice at once turned the balance of doubt, and the Amir forthwith decided to act honestly as being the best policy.

Azim Khan, in his view of the situation, accepted the arguments advanced by Sher Ali; acknowledged that as infidels we were the fair prey of Islam, and that as a conquering neighbour we were the enemy of the Afghan; and admitted that our adversity was their opportunity. But, at the same time, with a far-seeing discretion he warned the Amir to count well the cost and make sure of success before he committed himself to the alluring enterprise. He reminded his hearers that the British had already on a previous occasion found their way to Kabul when the Panjab lay between; and he pointed to their position now at the mouth of the Khybar. He agreed to the attack on Peshawar, provided the Amir was reasonably assured of success, but warned him, in the event of failure, to be prepared for the loss of his country. And this was enough to decide the Amir in the line of his future friendly policy.

Whilst this was the turn taken at Kabul, it was whispered in the Panjab—as is now no secret—that the highest authority in the province gravely entertained the intention of abandoning the territories we held across the Indus, and retiring to the east bank of the river. But, fortunately for the British in India, there were brave officers on the frontier, who knew the meaning and consequences of such a retrograde step, and who were prepared to take upon themselves the responsibility of refusing to execute the suicidal measure. To those six or seven undaunted hearts—all now gone from the scene of their daring, and some (General John Nicholson, Major Hugh James, Sir Herbert Edwardes, and Sir Sydney Cotton) long since passed away to their rest—England owes the safety of her Indian Empire through the storm of the mutiny. Now, whatever the merits of the arguments for or against the Indus as a frontier-line—and the question is one that was once more mooted at a later time—there can be no question of the impropriety of entertaining the idea at the time it was first advanced for serious consideration. The danger then threatening from the mere conception of such an idea was happily at once averted, but the fact of its production at all, and subsequent discussion as an unsettled question of state policy, has not been without influence in bringing about the complications preceding the present rupture between the Amir and the British Government, and has certainly stimulated his aspirations, not only for the recovery of the Indus provinces of Afghanistan, but for the restoration to Kabul of the territory held by the Durrani sovereign down to the river Jhelam, or, as is sometimes heard, down to Lahore itself—the frontier ceded to Ahmad Shah by the

Mughal emperor Muhammad Shah when he bought off the former's threatened attack upon Delhi by the bribe of a large subsidy and his own daughter in marriage. And all this to be effected with the promised aid of the Russian!

On the conclusion of peace with Persia —returning to our review of the course of events in Afghanistan—Herat was restored to Afghan rule in the person of Sardar Ahmad Khan, Barakzai, generally known as Sultan Jan. He was a brother of the Amir Dost Muhammad, and had been an active participator in the rebellion and massacre at Kabul in 1841, and at the time of his installation at Herat was known to be more—as regarded his political tendencies—in the interest of Persia than in that of the British Government. And this was presently exemplified by his coining in the name of the Persian Shah, and in his receiving and entertaining for some time the Russian mission under Khanikoff, on its way down the western frontier of Afghanistan to Sistan. The consignment of Herat to his charge—however much a necessity of the time and situation—proved a sore disappointment and inexplicable move to Dost Muhammad, and was viewed with discontent and alarm by his heir apparent at Kandahar. It was enough, however, for the Government of India that this frontier fortress and key of the country was in the keeping of a member of the ruling Barakzai family, for despite home jealousies and contentions, the place was unquestionably safer in such hands than in those of a foreigner.

With this settlement of the Herat difficulty, affairs in Afghanistan assumed a temporary lull. Lumsden's Mission returned to India, and our Native Agent remained permanently established at Kabul, whence he kept his own government informed of passing events. But the country was kept as close sealed as ever against access on the side of India, and the frontier relations between the two neighbour governments continued on their former footing—a jealous suspicion and exclusion on the part of the Amir, and a conciliatory forbearance and unnecessary submission to indignities on the part of the Government of India.

On the departure of the British Mission from Kandahar, the Sardar Ghulam Hydar Khan proceeded to Kabul, and died shortly after arrival there in July, 1858. Dost Muhammad then nominated his younger brother by the same mother—

Sardar Sher Ali Khan—as heir apparent in his stead, and duly informed the Government of India of the fact. This action of the Amir in determining the succession to the government in the line of the younger members of his family by a favourite wife, was held to be a defiance of the customs of the country and the acknowledged rights of primogeniture coupled with fitness, and gave rise to dissensions in the family and discontent amongst the nobles, who foresaw in the Amir's choice a repetition of the anarchy that followed upon the death of Tymur. The claims of his eldest sons, Muhammad Afzal, governor of Balkh, and Muhammad Azim, governor of Kurram, were urged upon the Amir by the nobles, with warnings of the confusion and bloodshed that would inevitably ensue after his death, should he persist in ignoring the just rights of proved and able governors. But Dost Muhammad was resolute in his determination, and turned a deaf ear to the counsels of his oldest adherents and well-wishers. In his ripe old age of over three-score and ten years, his death in the course of nature was an event that might occur at any time, and consequently the whole country was thrown into uncertainty, and parties were formed and reformed against the early expected day when the contest for the succession should commence in earnest. And this state of suspense and expectation disturbed the minds of his people, and for five years kept the country distracted by ever-changing and re-changing factions at court and parties in the provinces, together with a revived activity of intrigue with

Persia on the sides of Kandahar and Herat.

It was in this state of parties in the country, that Sardar Ahmad Khan died at Herat early in 1862, without an acknowledged successor to the government. One candidate after another claimed the rule, and each in turn appealed for support to the Persian governor of Mashhad, whilst an unsuccessful one hoisted the British flag as the symbol of his right. The interference of the Persian increased the confusion, and introduced an element of complication which at one time threatened a recurrence of the former difficulties with this important frontier fortress of Afghanistan; until the Amir, alarmed for the safety of the key of his house, set out to secure it in his own keeping. The opportunity was one he had patiently waited for, and it was his good fortune to find it before too late. Accompanied from Kabul by the heir apparent, the Amir reinforced his small army at Kandahar, and in May, 1863, after a siege of three weeks, was master of Herat. This was the last great act of the Amir Dost Muhammad Khan, and with it he closed his long and successful rule. He died in his camp under the walls of the fortress, on the 6th June, only a few days after its capture, aged seventy-six years.

The "Great Amir," *Amiri Kabir*, as he is generally styled by his own people, was a popular and successful ruler in his day, and a character greatly admired by the Afghans for his intrepidity, vigour, and general success in war; whilst his simple manners, free hospitality, and rough and ready justice, coupled with a ready intercourse with and free accessibility to his subjects of all classes, gained him the respect and affection of them all. Yet during his long reign he did nothing to improve the condition or advance the domestic welfare of his people, nor did he introduce a single measure of general benefit to the country. He kept it a close borough of Islam, stationary in the ignorance of the middle ages, and pervaded with the religious bigotry of that period; and to the close of his life defended that policy as the only one whereby to maintain the independence of the country. For his undisturbed reign and the general prosperity of his rule he is mainly indebted to the consistent support and recognition of the British Government, given as they were freely and without return, and supplemented as they were by a long enduring forbearance. His great merit is that he had the sense to perceive his own interest in the British alliance; and he reaped the fruits of his good judgment in the ultimate consolidation of his kingdom. But he was a barbarian nevertheless.

The last act of his reign—the recovery of Herat to the Government of Kabul—completed the consolidation of the state under an undivided authority. But this new and long desired state of the Barakzai rule was in its very initiation destined to undergo the fiery and perilous ordeal of civil war and domestic anarchy. The new Amir—Sher Ali Khan—had no sooner concluded the funeral ceremonies over the grave of his father at Herat than, leaving his youthful and able son Yacub Khan in charge of the place, he set out for Kabul, where, in September, 1863, he assumed the government as Amir. At no time a popular provincial governor, he assumed the reins of government with a character for severity and wilfulness that did not bode well for his tenure of the throne. He commenced his reign, however, with studied caution, conciliated the merchants by a reduction of the tariff, and gained the favour of the priesthood by an avowed hostility to the British, towards whom since his youth he had shown a marked antipathy.

Just at this time—towards the close of 1863—our troops were engaged in the prosecution of the Ambèla campaign, in the hills to the north of the Peshawar valley, against the Hindustani fanatics—our subjects, who had formed a seditious colony beyond the border at Malka on the Mahaban mountain—and it was at this juncture that Sher Ali announced to the Government of India his accession to the throne as Amir of Kabul, and expressed the hope of receiving its countenance and support. But considering that his subjects, excited by the priesthood, were at the very time flocking to swell the ranks of our opponents in the Ambèla hills, the hope expressed by Sher Ali seemed somewhat out of place, and the circumstance was brought to his notice by the officer then in political charge at Peshawar. That the Amir at this time had any great control over his subjects is doubtful. Anyhow the campaign was concluded early in the opening year with the destruction of the several positions attacked, and the defeat of the enemy, by the unaided force of the British arms, and without the least assistance, moral or other, from Sher Ali.

The new Amir was busy arranging his government and introducing reforms; and amongst others the reduction to the state pensions granted to some of the nobles—an indiscreet and untimely measure, which deprived him of the support of many powerful leaders of the people. The discontent produced by these innovations afforded his elder brothers the opportunity to advance their own interests, and Muhammad Afzal and Muhammad Azim very soon secured a large party in favour of their cause.

Azim, the governor of Kurram, was the first to rebel, but an army being promptly sent to coerce him, he abandoned his government, and sought shelter in British territory. Presently Afzal, the governor of Balkh, revolted, and against him Sher Ali marched in person with a considerable army. After some indecisive collisions he inveigled Afzal into his power on a promise of fair adjustment of their dispute, and then, in violation of his oath, cast him into prison—an act of treachery condemned even by Afghans. This occurred in August, 1864. And so commenced the civil war in Kabul, which lasted five years, and ended with the final recovery of the throne by Sher Ali. It is unnecessary and unprofitable here to recite the complex changes of parties and events which during this period chequered the board of Afghan history with a maze of intricacies. It is enough for our purpose to note only the most salient features of the civil war, in so far as they affected the relations of the state with the Government of India.

After Sher Ali had secured Afzal as his captive, he set out after his son, Abdurrahman Khan, who had raised the whole province of Balkh in rebellion, and driving him from place to place, pacified the country as he proceeded. Meanwhile Azim, disgusted at his failure to get assistance from the British, towards whom he had always observed a disposition of friendliness, made his way through Swat and Badakhshan to Balkh, and there joining his nephew Abdurrahman, soon raised a strong party, and releasing Afzal, attacked Kabul in March, 1866. The Amir Sher Ali was defeated and fled to Kandahar, whilst Muhammad Afzal entered Kabul as Amir on the 21st May. And he was duly recognized as such by the Government of India. He died very suddenly—his death being attributed to cholera—on the 7th October, 1867, and is now reckoned the second Amir of Afghanistan. He was succeeded by his brother Muhammad Azim as Amir, but he was not as such officially recognized by the Government of India, and he is not now reckoned amongst the Amirs of Afghanistan.

Sher Ali in the meantime, after two unsuccessful attempts to recover his throne from Kandahar, and hopeless of aid from the British, proceeded to Herat and sought the help of Persia. Returning from this to Kandahar, he organized a force and made another effort to regain Kabul, but was signally defeated in a decisive battle fought near Kalati Ghilzai on the 22nd January, 1867. In this battle he lost his favourite son Muhammad Ali, a youth of remarkable talents and great promise. He was killed in single combat by his uncle Muhammad Amin Khan—full brother of Sher Ali—who himself was then cut down by the attendant soldiers. His defeat and the loss of these two near relatives powerfully affected Sher

Ali, who fell back upon Kandahar, and shut himself up to mourn over his losses. He is said to have quite lost his senses for a time through excess of grief. The intelligence, however, of Azim's accession to the throne as Amir roused him out of the lethargy into which he had fallen, and he set out for Herat, to make another attempt upon Kabul from the side of Turkistan. But here also he was defeated by Abdurrahman, and at the same time lost Kandahar to Sarwar Khan, the son of Azim.

Finally, after negotiating with Russian agents in Bukhara, and collecting what money he could in the country, Sher Ali repaired to Herat, and here, getting aid from Persia and Russia, he once more organized a force for the recovery of his throne. He secretly bought over to his side Ismail Khan, who was with Abdurrahman in Balkh, and himself advanced by way of Kandahar, sending his son Yacub Khan ahead with the main army. All this revival and activity on the part of Sher Ali commenced after the interview of Yacub with the Shah of Persia on the occasion of his visit to Mashhad in 1867.

Yacub captured Kandahar from Sarwar in April, 1868, and on the 10th of the following month Sher Ali entered the city in state amidst the acclamations of the people, who had been terribly oppressed by Sarwar Khan. From this point, with Yacub operating in advance, Sher Ali steadily made good his advance towards Kabul, and by September established himself in all the country up to Ghazni. His position here drew Azim from the capital to oppose him, and Ismail then descending from Balkh, took Kabul city by a *coup-de-main* in the name of Sher Ali, and laid siege to the Bala Hissar, held by Shamsuddin Khan on the part of Azim. At this critical juncture Azim, whose rule was horribly oppressive and cursed by the people, was deserted by all but a few trusty personal attendants, and seeing the game lost, he fled towards Persia by way of Sistan. He died at Shahrûd on the high road to Tehran from Mashhad, in the summer of 1869. With the flight of Azim the road to Kabul for Sher Ali was clear, and he was welcomed back by the citizens as a deliverer from the tyrants who had squeezed and ground them to the last extremity to meet their current expenses.

Once more in possession of his throne, Sher Ali was by no means secure against further assault, for though Afzal had been removed by death, and Azim by the desertion of his party and his own flight from the country, still there was Abdurrahman (the son and heir of the Amir Afzal, who was considered the rightful successor of the Amir Dost Muhammad) yet at large and an avowed claimant of the throne, the recovery of which it was supposed he would attempt with the aid of Russia. Whatever entanglements Sher Ali may have had with Persia and Russia, and whatever may have been the hopes of Abdurrahman from the latter, there is no doubt that at this time, as Sher Ali approached Kabul, he was extremely anxious to secure the recognition and support of the British Government, and lost no time in communicating his desires to that government. His overtures being received in a friendly spirit, Sher Ali at once threw himself upon the support and protection of the British, and, leaving his newly recovered capital in charge of his son Yacub, set out for India in February, 1869, to meet the new Viceroy, Lord Mayo, at Amballa. He was accompanied by his youthful son, and nominated heir apparent, Abdulla Jan, and a small retinue of court officials, of whom his Prime Minister, Nùr Muhammad Shah, was the most important personage.

The reception accorded by Lord Mayo to Sher Ali was highly honourable and hospitable in the extreme, and did much to soften those bitter feelings—feelings which he took no care to conceal—which possessed his mind on first arrival, as the result of our abstention from intermediation in the contest for the succession. The treatment Sher Ali received on this occasion was most gratifying to his natural pride, and—although the extravagant demands he put forward, with nothing conceded in return on his own part, were not acceded to—he was on the whole pleased with his visit, and returned to Kabul a made man, and full of all sorts of plans of reformation. He took away with him rich gifts in arms and money, and, more valuable than all, the good-will and recognition of the British Government. Affairs at Kabul, and thence all over Afghanistan, at once, as if by magic, assumed a settled aspect under the newly-acquired prestige of the fortune-favoured Amir. His enemies everywhere accepted the altered situation, renounced their ambitious schemes, ceased their factious intrigues, and submitted with unexpected resignation to the rapid changes and innovations which, in the first burst of his zeal for reform, Sher Ali set to work introducing into the administration of his government immediately after his return from India. The sense of injustice suffered at our hands during the late civil war, by our abandonment of his admitted rights, and the recognition of the temporary success of his rival, though never referred to by Sher Ali without reproach and complaint, seemed to have been greatly mitigated, if not removed entirely by his handsome reception in India. The disappointment caused by the rejection of his very large requests was taken in good part and treated as a hope deferred. And the *rapprochement* between the two governments, thus happily inaugurated, was genuine and cordial, and full of promise for the future, till nipped in the bud by the blight of the Sistan arbitration.

Sher Ali at the time of his visit to India was solicitous, not so much for the safety of his own position at Kabul—of which he was assured by the removal from the scene of his two most powerful adversaries, and by the final recognition of the British—as he was for the security of his country against the approaching danger of the Russian advance in Turkistan. At the time that Dost Muhammad annexed Balkh the Russian outpost in Turkistan was still no farther advanced than the lower course of the Jaxartes. But by 1854, when Kandahar was added to Kabul, the Russians had taken up positions at Ac Masjid and Almati or Vernui. And by the time that Herat was recovered to Kabul, the Russians were closing up the line between their advanced posts, and completed the operation by the capture of Tashkand in 1864. Finally, during the course of the Afghan civil war, the Russians extended their conquests to Samarkand and the Bukhara.

line of frontier at Jam; and immediately sought the concession of Charjoe on the Oxus as an advanced military outpost.

The rapid progress of the Russian arms over the petty states of Turkistan could not fail to inspire the Amir with alarm, and misgivings as to where the wave of onward rolling conquest would end, or how soon it might reach his own frontier line on the Oxus. His alarm on this score was real, and his desire for the assurance of our aid in the time of need very earnest. He saw that his own interests in this matter of the security and defence of the northern boundary of Afghanistan were identical with our own, and he therefore looked on his proposal for the conclusion of an offensive and defensive treaty between Kabul and India as a point on which there could be no demur or difficulty. Though at the time disappointed in the failure of this desire to be thus assured of his future safety against Russian encroachment, Sher Ali did not abandon the hope of its ultimate attainment, and meanwhile accepted the good offices of the British Government in the matter of coming to a diplomatic understanding with the Government of Russia on the subject of the recognition and respect of the northern boundaries of the Afghan territories. His confidence in the British Government was at this time complete, and his conduct frank and upright, as evinced by his passing on to the Government of India all communications received by him from the Russian authorities in Turkistan for information, and for guidance as to the reply he should give. He, in fact, put himself completely in our hands in the matter of this negotiation, yet he would not then consent to receive British officers as political residents in his country, though he held out the hope of his being able to do so at some future and not long distant time, after the friendship now so promisingly commenced had had time to mature and smooth away existing animosities and suspicions.

And in justice to Sher Ali, it must be admitted that—in spite of his disappointment in the matter of the treaty, as well as in that of the recognition of his nominee as heir apparent—he did to some extent, though small and gradual as it was, make an effort to cultivate a freer intercourse with India, and as an earnest of his new policy of friendship with us, relaxed the heretofore rigid exclusion of Indians and Europeans from Afghan soil. During the three or four years following the return of Sher Ali to Kabul from his interview with Lord Mayo, a large number of Indians, both Hindu and Mussulman, and three or four Englishmen visited Kabul in the course of trade or business, and with perfect safety. This promising aspect of Sher Ali's attitude and sentiments towards us was not, most unfortunately, destined to last long. There were two circumstances which at this time occurred to mar the even tenour of the relations between Sher Ali and us.

Unaffected by the refusal of the Government of India to recognize the heir of his choice, Sher Ali on his return to Kabul proclaimed his favourite son Abdulla Jan, then a delicate and not very bright boy of eight years of age, as heir apparent, and to check opposition made his nobles and courtiers swear to acknowledge and support him. This choice of the Amir roused the jealousy of Yacub Khan, an elder son by another mother, who, considering the active part he had taken in recovering Kabul for his father, claimed the succession as his right both by birth and by state service. But Sher Ali, probably better informed than Yacub's partisans in India of the youth's political tendencies and intrigue entanglements, adhered to his resolve and took care to hedge round his nominee with every means of strength. And to this he was driven by the rebellion and flight of Yacub to Herat, and the sympathy and partiality evinced towards him in India, as well as by a considerable section of his own people. In this state of the case, and with the view to maintain quiet in his own country, Sher Ali again sought the recognition of the British Government in favour of Abdulla Jan, but without success, and this unwillingness on their part to meet his views for the final settlement of this question, produced in his mind a doubt as to their sincerity, and certainly checked the progress of the *rapprochement* between the two governments. At the same time that this difficulty was pending, the question of Sistan was under consideration.

The settlement of the negotiation regarding the northern boundaries of Afghanistan which the Amir had entrusted in full confidence to the British Government resulted so much to his benefit by the definition of the Oxus boundary and the enclosure within the line of the Afghan frontier of the yet unappropriated districts of Badakhshan and Wakhan, that Sher Ali had no cause to suppose his confidence misplaced, nor indeed did he so think. On the contrary, apart from his discontent in the matter of our views regarding the family dispute with Yacub, he confided his interests in the dispute with Persia regarding the possession of Sistan to our hands, with unabated trust in our good-will and justice, and, foregoing at our instance a direct appeal to force, consented to submit the question to the arbitration of the British Government. In thus committing his interests in that region to our decision, so convinced was Sher Ali of the justness of his claim to the territory in dispute with Persia, that it seems it never occurred to him that his foregone conclusions might possibly be reversed in the issue.

In the prosecution of this arbitration Sir F. J. Goldsmith, accompanied by a staff of British officers and a Persian agent, proceeded to Sistan from the side of Persia, as Arbitrator, and Colonel (now Sir R. F.) Pollock, accompanied by an assistant and an Afghan agent, proceeded to the same destination from the side of India, as exponent of the Amir's case; and both parties met in Sistan in March, 1872. As a result of the investigation conducted on the spot, the territory which had belonged to Afghanistan ever since the establishment of the Durrani empire by Ahmad Shah, and had been seized by Persia only during the confusion of the civil war in Afghanistan which followed upon the death of Dost Muhammad in 1863, was declared to belong to Persia by right of actual possession; and a boundary-line was drawn across a map of the province as the limit beyond which neither Persian nor Afghan was to transgress.

The movement of the Persians towards this important corner of Afghanistan had long been contemplated, and intrigues had long been set on foot and worked quietly and perseveringly to gain a footing in the territory without the employment of force, and not—as was found to be the case—altogether unsuccessfully. But it was only after the journey this way of the Russian Mission under Khanikoff that Persia boldly announced her claim to the territory, and it was only after Yacub Khan's interview with the Shah at Mashhad that military possession was taken of the western parts of the province by Persian troops. Whatever the rights of the question, or merits of the arbitration, there is no doubt that the decision given against the Amir highly incensed him against us, and at once completed the revulsion in his sentiments of newly born good-will towards us (which had already been commenced by the part taken by us in Sher Ali's quarrel with his son Yacub), and at a stroke undid all that had been done since the Amballa meeting, to cement a good understanding and cordial co-operation between the two governments for the advancement and development of their mutual relations and interests.

Sher Ali felt, in the decision given, and —on his remonstrance—upheld against him by us, that we had inflicted a grievous injury upon him in respect to a most important strategical point of his country, and had besides dragged his honour in the dust at the feet of the Persian—to him, as an orthodox Sunni, the accursed Shiah.

But putting aside the question of his honour and offended dignity, Sher Ali argued that the position accorded to Persia in Sistan gravely compromised the authority of his rule in that out-of-the-way and remote quarter, and, moreover, very seriously threatened the security of his western frontier. For, by surrendering this portion of his line of defence in that direction, he lost a position on the maintenance of which the safety of Herat largely depended. In fact, Persia—which in his view was the same as Russia—had, by this decision of the question, succeeded in driving a wedge into the south-western granary of Afghanistan, to the splitting asunder of the integrity of the frontier, and the tapping of the line of communication between Kandahar and Herat, and the dominance of both these provinces in time of war. Further, he considered our arbitration so unreasonable—even on the grounds on which we put the case and its decision before him—that he was at a loss to account for what seemed a manifest stultification of our own arguments. He suspected our collusion with Russia, or our fear of her, and condemned the whole business in no unmeasured terms. In his own court he never alluded to the subject without losing his temper, and vowed repeatedly that we should never forget the day on which we thus sold him, for he would never forgive us.

Sher Ali was in this discontented state of mind, sulky and sore at the somewhat peremptory manner in which his criticisms of our Sistan arbitration had been snubbed, when the Government of India, towards the close of 1873, informed him that a mission of British officers under Mr. (now Sir D. P.) Forsyth would return to India from Kashghar by way of Balkh and Kabul, and requested his good offices for their protection and honourable treatment on the road through his territories. At any other time of smoother diplomatic relations between the two governments such a request, preferred without previous consultation and understanding, might have been entertained and arranged to the satisfaction of both parties, but made as, and when, it was no other than a negative reply or shuffling excuse could have been expected; especially as Sher Ali had already expressed, rather curtly, his objection to British officers entering his country, and had complained of one who had passed from Persia to India by Herat and Kandahar without his permission or consent.

This untoward occurrence added to the wrath of the Amir the suspicion that we were overriding his proper authority, and the suspicion thus aroused was presently confirmed by the intervention of the Government of India on behalf of Yacub Khan, whom the Amir, having enticed to Kabul from Herat, cast into prison for rebellion against his authority and conspiracy against the throne. This act of the Government of India was viewed by Sher Ali as an unwarrantable intrusion upon his domestic concerns, and an interference in the internal affairs of the country, which was contrary to our repeated assurances; and he resented the interposition with some warmth. This cause of grievance had hardly passed away, when by some oversight, a communication was made direct, and without previous reference to the Amir, with his frontier

Governor in Badakhshan—a trivial accident, merely a letter of thanks for attention and civility shown to a party detached from the Kashghar Mission. But in the then state of his temper, it did not escape the notice of Sher Ali. These unlucky miscarriages of official routine, with others of minor importance, formed the subject of very warm discussion in the court of Kabul, and were unanimously condemned as a departure from the policy of non-interference heretofore observed and confirmed by Lord Mayo. Both Sher Ali and his courtiers were now thoroughly mistrustful of our intentions, and confirmed in the revulsion of their friendly disposition and sentiments towards us. The confidence at first displayed by the submission of all Russian correspondence to the Government of India was replaced by a strict reserve, and the withholdment of all intelligence concerning the events passing on and beyond the distant frontiers of Afghanistan; whilst the correspondence through our native agent at Kabul was very guarded and concise, and the agent himself kept under a strict surveillance.

This hitch in the even tenour of our relations with Sher Ali was at once seized upon by the Russian authorities at Tashkand to ingratiate themselves in his favour, and their heretofore rejected advances being now encouraged by him, a continuous succession of Russian agents and emissaries began to pass and repass between Tashkand and Kabul. Beyond the mere fact of the arrival and departure of the more prominent amongst them, we knew nothing whatever of their sayings and doings, or the object of their comings and goings.

Whilst this was the freedom of access to Afghanistan on the side of Russia, the passes on the side of India were watched with vigilant care, and, in fact, practically closed to all except Afghan subjects going and coming in the course of their commercial business with India.

Sher Ali had now, 1875, to all intents and purposes thrown over the English, to try a turn of the Russian friendship. The line of conduct now adopted by Sher Ali—an attitude of studied reserve and estrangement towards the British Government, and one of lively intercourse and *rapprochement* with that of Russia—could not fail to awaken us in India to the perils such a course, if allowed to continue, was sure to bring upon us. It could not fail to rouse the government to a proper safeguarding of the interests of the Empire upon the frontiers held by him. In fact, the attitude now assumed by Sher Ali towards the British Government was a subversion of the heretofore existing order of relations between the two governments since their connexion as neighbours after the conquest of the Panjab, and a new departure upon lines tending in a diametrically opposite direction to those hitherto followed. That the Amir has any solid grounds of justification for this sudden change of front there is—whatever the shadow of semblance—not the least reality of substance. In dwelling upon the grievances alleged by him as above mentioned, Sher Ali has taken an entirely one-sided and personal view of the case, and exposed the secret of his own ambitions which have grown out of the fostering care and maintenance he has received—gratuitously and liberally, without any return, even the smallest, on his own part—from the very government whose friendship—so long benefited by, to the consolidation of his kingdom, and his own establishment on the throne—he now spurns. Sher Ali, in the blindness of his ambition and the excess of his pride, ignores the benefits he has received from the British Government, and forgets that but for the consistent countenance and very material support afforded by that powerful neighbour on successive occasions of domestic peril, there would not at this moment have been the united Afghanistan made and defined to his hand for him—a country consolidated and strengthened for the defence of the Empire of which it forms the frontier province; not, as he would now use it, to be a weapon against the paramount sovereign.

The countenance and support which have been uniformly afforded by the British Government to that of Afghanistan ever since the annexation of the Panjab has undoubtedly not been entirely disinterested, but it has been, up to the time we are now considering, most undoubtedly advantageous to the mutual interests of the two governments, which from their position as neighbours in part of an integral whole, cannot sever themselves from the bonds of a natural connexion and union, whether the tie be considered from a geographical, national, or political point of view. More than this, the sum of the advantages conferred by the paramount government has preponderated greatly in favour of the weaker state, and, raising it out of a state of anarchy and dismemberment, has brought it to a condition fitting for the successful development of its own internal resources under an enlightened government and civilized administration on the part of the ruler. That this orderly settlement and material development of Afghanistan as an independent frontier-state in alliance with the British Empire in India has been the object aimed at by our Government, is clearly manifested throughout the course of its dealings with the rulers of that country; and with so scrupulous an attention to their national prejudices, and so conciliatory a deference to their lawless proclivities that it has systematically abstained from interference in their home affairs—has abstained from pressing very necessary reforms upon them, and from exacting a return in compensation for the support it afforded to them. Even more, it has patiently endured the ignominy of a rigid exclusion of its subjects from their territory, and of the denial of justice to the murderers of its unoffending subjects—amongst the number several British officers assassinated within their own limits by Afghan subjects crossing the border.

With such forbearance towards the Afghan Amir our Government has been compelled in self-defence to resist by force and punish from time to time the raids of his independent tribesmen along the frontier, and during the thirty years of its tenure of the position there, to carry—large and small together—more than that number of punitory expeditions into the hills held by them. But with all this we have laid no restrictions upon the intercourse of the Amir's people with India. They pass and they repass, even in this time of active war with Sher Ali, unquestioned and unhindered, and in British India find more freedom, security, and justice than they do in their own country. Further, apart from the very considerable material aid granted freely to the Amir, our Government affords the bounty of its hospitality to scores of Aghan princelings and nobles who have been exiled from their home by the Afghan Amir for his own peace and their safety. In short, if we strike a balance of the account between ourselves and the Amir, we shall find Sher Ali very considerably in our debt. Let us look at the main items. We have twice rescued Herat from the Persian by force of arms, and restored the place to the Afghan at a cost to ourselves of several millions of money and some thousands of lives. We have from time to time eased the pecuniary necessities of the Amir by free gifts of money, aggregating half a million sterling. We have given him thirty thousand muskets and two batteries of rifled artillery with their proper munitions. We have trained drill-instructors and officers for him in the ranks of our Indian army, and we have provided him with skilled artisans for his gun-cap and arms manufactories. Finally, we have sheltered and restrained dozens of exiled members of his family and others, his sworn enemies and rivals. What has the Amir done for us in return for these concessions and favours? Nothing, simply nothing but the postponement of the day of his enmity. His repeated refusal to admit our officers to his country, his steady denial of justice against the crimes of his subjects in our territories, and his continuous demands for greater and more unrestricted assistance, are samples of the kind of return he made for our friendship, till finally, taking offence at the settlement of a negotiation entrusted to us for decision, he estranged himself from us, and made a grievance of some unfortunate and easily remedied accidents of official routine, to persevere in a mood of ill-temper and rudeness towards the powerful neighbour who had made his country what it was, and his own position in it what he has proved himself unworthy of holding.

It was in this condition of the relations between the two governments, and in consequence of the unshaken attitude of estrangement persevered in by Sher Ali, that the Government of India resolved, as a precautionary measure, to take up the position at Quetta which had long been contemplated, and to which it was entitled by treaty rights with the Khan of Balochistan, but which it had hitherto abstained from doing out of deference to the sensitiveness of the Amir. At the same time the Government endeavoured to negotiate with the Amir for an amicable settlement of the existing differences and a more satisfactory and secure arrangement for the future; and with this object in view were prepared to grant Sher Ali the several requests he had on previous occasions submitted to the Government of India, such as the recognition of Abdulla Jan, the son of his choice, as heir apparent; the conclusion of a treaty, offensive and defensive on equal terms; and the free grant of a very handsome sum of money, with a regular subsidy besides. Had Sher Ali accepted the terms now offered, he would have secured lasting safety, and peace, and prosperity to Afghanistan, but the breach between himself and us was already too wide for him to care to bridge it over. The delicate task of this difficult business fell to the skilful hands of Lord Lytton, the newly installed Viceroy, who, in May, 1876, shortly after his assumption of office, despatched a distinguished native officer, one of his own aides-de-camp, to Kabul with a friendly letter to the Amir, and explanations regarding the important matters then affecting the interests of the two governments. It soon became apparent that the reception of the Viceroy's messenger at Kabul boded no good as the result of future negotiation, and consequently the occupation of Quetta was proceeded with, and a detachment of native troops of the Indian army arrived there to garrison the place in October.

As a result of the correspondence between the Viceroy and the Amir, Sher Ali sent his Prime Minister, Nur Muhammad Shah, as envoy to Peshawar, there to meet Sir Lewis Pelly, envoy of the Government of India, and there to discuss the several matters then before the two governments for adjustment. Although Sher Ali had taken no notice of the Viceroy's polite attention in inviting his Highnest to grace with his presence the imperial assemblage about to be held at Delhi on the 1st January, 1877, his envoy arrived at Peshawar shortly after the conclusion of that august ceremony. He was accompanied by Mirakhor (Master of, or Lord of the Stable) Ahmad Khan, an important court official, notoriously hostile to the British in particular, and all European infidels in general, and a small retinue of attendants. With the envoy came the British agent at Kabul, a portly gentleman, eternally telling his beads and gabbling his litanies to the interruption of his speech and distraction of his attention from business, and with the not very flattering habit of hawking and spitting after converse with the unbeliever.

The conference between the two envoys was entered upon without loss of time, and it soon became apparent that the Afghan (apart from the experience of his previous dealings with the Government of India, his knowledge of the diverse views held in high quarters, and his acquaintance with the fussiness of frontier officials who would have opinions of their own) had received positive instructions from his master on the score of rejecting the basis on which the negotiations he had come for were to commence. He wasted his breath in tedious repetitions of the Amir's grievances and wrongs at our hands, and his disgust at our shilly-shally policy; and he concluded his rambling arguments with the rejection of the basis (the reception of British officers as political agents on the Afghan frontiers) which it was understood Sher Ali had accepted before sending his envoy. This decision of the Afghan envoy closed the conference, without the stage of negotiation being approached, and it was evidently intended to be a final and decisive break with the British, as confirmed by the action of the Amir at this time. Whilst his envoy was at Peshawar on a friendly mission to the British Government, Sher Ali, at Kabul, was busy preaching a *jahad*, or "religious war," against it, and summoning his subjects to join the army he had assembled at Jalalabad. And this too without the move of a single regiment on our part towards the frontier. The Afghan envoy was in very failing health at the time he came to Peshawar, and he died there shortly after the conclusion of his business, in March, 1877.

And so ended the last attempt on our part to renew amicable relations with the Amir of Kabul. The breach between Sher Ali and the British was now complete and hopeless. After this Sher Ali took possession of the fort of Ali Masjid in the Khybar Pass, and garrisoning it with his own troops, put guards upon all the roads and passes towards Kabul, and, in fact, closed his country entirely against British subjects on the side of India. At the same time, he issued strict orders for the minutest precautions to be taken against any intelligence from his country reaching India, and severely punished and harassed those of his subjects who were suspected of being friendly to us. Yet all this time, and up to the time of the rebuff of Chamberlain's mission at the Khybar, so great was the indifference of our forbearance, that Sher Ali's postmaster and namesake was left alone undisturbed at Peshawar, to send his master the daily telegrams from Europe, and our own doings in India.

Of the course of events in Afghanistan since this time—about the middle of 1877—we have no reliable or connected account. It was known that after breaking off his relations with us, Sher Ali at once turned his thoughts to the Russians, and courted the advances on their side which he had so long kept at arm's length. But what the nature of his communications and negotiations with them now was, remained a mystery. Bazar reports were rife enough, and the gossip brought down by Afghan traders of the sayings and doings of the Kabul court were soon the theme of discussion in every city of India. In the midst of all that was heard there was much that was interesting and instructive, as indicating the influence and effects upon the people of Afghanistan of thirty years' independent contact with British rule; and much that showed that the people as a whole entirely disapproved of Sher Ali's conduct towards the British Government. The Englishman, officially denounced at Kabul as the infidel and all that was vile, was spoken of by these people, away from the restraint of their rulers, as the patron of justice and the herald of peace and prosperity. Whilst the Amir Sher Ali, at no time a popular ruler, was upbraided for his ingratitude and faithlessness, abused for his tyrannous oppression, and viewed as a traitor for admitting the Russian into Afghanistan. In fact, the public opinion of the country was divided into two great camps. In the one, headed by the Amir, were the nobles and their clansmen, the clergy, and government officials of all ranks but the lowest: in fact, in this camp were mustered all who held authority, place, and position in the country. In the other headed by the great merchants and some depressed nobles, were the trading community, the industrial classes in the cities and the agricultural populations in the villages around them. The first was bound to maintain its position at all hazards. The second sighed for relief from the burdens oppressing it, and looked with a favouring eye upon the British; whilst apart from both parties were the hill-tribes, who cared only to preserve their independence. The classes in the latter camp were wearied and worn by the exactions and oppressions of their rulers, and were ready to welcome any new comer. They knew the British by reputation, and some of them by experience. Under British rule there was law and protection, and a man's liberty and earnings were his own—blessings they had heard of, but to which they were strangers in their own country. They had heard of the Russians, and knew them by reputation as a fierce and powerful people, who sided with the native rulers in grinding and squeezing the people. They knew nothing of the Russian rule in Turkistan, but they did know British rule in India; and they also knew that the prosperity of their country depended upon its trade with India, despite the road-tolls, customs-fees, and official exactions hampering it in their own limits. In short they liked the English rule, considered themselves British subjects, and longed for the day when the *Sarkár* (government) should take their country.

The classes in the former camp, by no means blind to the spread of knowledge amongst their people through their commerce with India, and the wonderful tales they brought back of its railways, bazar activity, and commercial prosperity, of its security, order, and liberty, knew that ignorance could not prevail for long, and that the result of comparison would be the growth of discontent and the necessity for reformation. But the sweets of despotism and irresponsibility are not easily surrendered; and hence the exclusive and restrictive policy pursued by the Government; hence the persistent refusal to receive British officers as political agents—for fear, as was repeatedly stated by the Afghan envoy at Peshawar, that their example would make the people dissatisfied with their own rulers; and hence, too, the preference now shown by Sher Ali for the Russian. It is stated on excellent authority that Sher Ali has recently often avowed in his public audiences at Kabul that he would sooner lose his country than see his subjects drawn away from his control by a preference for the British system of rule.

In fact, so long as the Amir could keep

us out of his country, and remain undisturbed in his despotism, he was willing to court our friendship and get out of us what he could. And in this policy there is no doubt that his people some years back coincided. The progress of time, however, has worked changes both in the political situation and in the popular sentiment in Afghanistan. The rapid advances made by Russia in recent years towards the Afghan frontier has of itself rendered it necessary that we should have a free and safe communication with that country, and assure ourselves by trustworthy and responsible agents of the integrity and security of its territories, and of the freedom of its people from Russian interference and intrigue. Whilst, at the same time, the increased growth of trade relations between the Afghans and Indians has rendered it incumbent upon us to protect their interests. For the trade of Afghanistan is with Hindustan, and has been so from time immemorial; and it is on this trade that the prosperity of the country depends. This trade cannot be diverted from its ancient channels, nor stopped even for a short time, without bringing ruin upon the country; because the productions of Afghanistan are also the productions of Persia and Bukhara—her staple exports are also their staple exports; and because the requirements of Afghanistan, her imports, are only from India, and can be profitably obtained only from India. The trade relations of Afghanistan, in short, bind her to India as strongly as do her national affinities, and political necessities. These facts are well known to the Afghans, and fully appreciated by them, however much it may suit their rulers to set them aside for the advancement of personal ambition.

Sher Ali, when he severed his connexion with the Government of India after the Peshawar conference, had no intention of immediately throwing himself into the arms of Russia. He hated and feared the Russian even more than he did the English, and was determined to the utmost of his power to keep both alike out of his territory as long as he possibly could. He knew perfectly well that his own best interests and those of his people were on the side of India and of the British, and not on the side of Persia or of Turkistan—of the Persian or the Russian. But he considered that he was indispensable to us; that we could not do without his friendship; and that if he only brought sufficient pressure to bear upon us, we should be obliged to give in and accept his terms. He encouraged the Russian advances, and shut up his country to us in the hope of intimidating us into concessions and overtures for a renewal of friendly relations, counting still upon the forbearance and conciliation we had shown on former occasions. And when he found that he had gone too far, and overshot the mark, his pride carried him farther away upon the false track, and he allowed himself to be entoiled in the web of Russian intrigue and seduction.

In this course Sher Ali was doubtless, seeing his own failure to coerce us, to some extent influenced by the course of events in Europe in connexion with the Russo-Turkish war, the incidents and successive phases of which were watched and discussed with the keenest interest in Kabul. During the progress of the war, and long before he had clearly identified himself with the Russian interest, Sher Ali received an envoy from the Sultan of Turkey, warning him against the Russian as the declared enemy of Islam, and advising him to make up his differences with the British Government, which was the well-wisher and protector of all Muhammadans. This at least was the ostensible errand of the Turkish envoy. But Khulùsi Effendi, if there be any reliance on popular rumour, drew such a picture at Kabul of the perfidy of England in deserting her ancient ally in the hour of his peril and distress, that Sher Ali was rather more inclined than otherwise towards the Russian. After this, the subject of the Russian alliance was spoken of more favourably at court, and discussed more freely than ever—with Russian agents and emissaries in the place to give the turn and furnish arguments in favour of their side—whilst the timidity of England was set down to conscious weakness and decay.

The merits of the two Great Powers were discussed seriatim, and the balance struck in favour of Russia. England, argued the Amir's advisers, was a selfish power, working only for the advancement of her own interests. It was true that since the Shah Shuja' episode she had assisted the Barakzai; but this was as much to her own advantage as to the benefit of the Afghan, since the interests of both were identical in the preservation of the country as an independent state. In short, where they did not see their own immediate interests affected, they did not trouble, or care to trouble, themselves on behalf of the Afghan. How did they treat the Amir during the civil war for the succession after the death of Dost Muhammad? Was it a fair or a friendly act to acknowledge as Amir the successful rival against the claims and rights of the acknowledged heir? How did they treat Sher Ali after he succeeded in recovering his "God-granted" throne and went to India to meet the Viceroy? Did they accede to any of the requests he preferred for the recognition of his chosen heir, or the conclusion of a treaty, or the grant of a subsidy? No, the English looked to their own interests and discarded those of the Amir. How did they treat the dignity of the Amir in sending their agent without his knowledge to his Governor of Badakhshan? Was that a right procedure on the part of one friendly government towards another? What was their conduct in the matter of the Amir's punishment of his rebellious son Yacub Khan? Was that an adherence to their repeated assurances of an abstention from interference in the domestic affairs of Afghanistan? How did they settle the Sistan question? Was giving away the Amir's territory to the Persian, and "blackening his face" before the world, a just settlement or honourable discharge of the duty they undertook for us? What is their move to Quetta? Do they mean to take Kandahar from us? And what is their last dealing with us? Is it fair to demand the concession of the location of their officers in our frontier towns before proceeding with negotiation? What are we to do with a government which treats us thus? Who encouraged us to raise an army, and gave us arms for the purpose? And now that we have raised a large army for the defence of their frontiers and India, why do they refuse us help to maintain it? Is this fair dealing? This is our experience of the British.

Russia, on the other hand—though equally the infidel, "God's curse upon them both!"—has done us no injury. We know her as a great, a powerful, and a victorious nation of whom England is afraid, and at whose growing strength she is alarmed and disconcerted. If England felt herself able to oppose Russia, why did she reject the appeals of the distressed Amirs of Khocand, and Bukhara, and Khiva, and refuse them her support and encouragement? What has come of her alliance and treaty with Atalic Ghazi? And what is the fate of Kashghar now?

Was England able to stop Russia in the war against the Sultan? Then, why did she desert her old ally? Was Sebastopol a victory or a defeat? No, England cannot withstand Russia. She cannot withstand her here without us, and yet she does not value our aid. Then Russia is our game. She means to attack India, and she will for her own purposes help us to reconquer our lost territories there. This is our chance, and in Russia our hope now centres. The Russian rule, besides, is preferable to that of the British, who depress the nobility and raise the mob; whereas Russia leaves the nobility to rule their people after their own fashion, and requires only loyalty and revenue. Let us then vote for Russia.

With arguments such as these the court of Kabul balanced England against Russia, and turned the scales in favour of the latter. But besides all these there was another motive which was not without weight at this crisis in inducing Sher Ali to cast in his lot with Russia. He was well aware that when Atalic Ghazi in 1864-5 established himself as an independent ruler in Kashghar, he sought to secure himself against Russia—into whose hands his native country of Tashkand had passed before he entered upon his career of conquest in Chinese Turkistan, and of whose empire he was consequently a subject—by getting himself acknowledged as a feudatory of the Sultan of Turkey; a project in which he was favoured with the influence and moral support of the Government of India. Sher Ali was also aware that it was the aim of Atalic Ghazi, after he assumed the title of Amir Yacub Beg under the flag of Turkey, to effect a confederation of the states of Central Asia under the same flag; and he foresaw what his own fate would be if this scheme were carried out, for he would then have no alternative but to lapse into a feudatory himself—and, more than merely probable, of the British Government. The danger of this, so far as Sher Ali was concerned, was yet remote at that time; but for Russia the mere conception of such a scheme was a near and pressing danger, and one that required immediate tackling. And this was done by Russia dealing her blow straight at the head. The diplomatic skill, the political sagacity, and the courageous action of Russia for the aversion of this vital danger to her empire in Asia, won—as it well might—the admiration of Sher Ali, and Russia's success so far in the enterprise has increased his confidence in her prestige.

And with all these causes at work it is noways strange that Sher Ali in July last welcomed a Russian Mission to Kabul.

All that passed at this time between Sher Ali and the Russians was kept so profoundly secret that in India we had no knowledge of the approaching Mission until it had already arrived at Kabul, and for several days enjoyed the hospitality of the Amir. The Russians were treated at Kabul with the greatest distinction, reviews were held in their honour, and the chiefs and representatives of the people were summoned from all parts of the country to meet the new friends of the Amir, the new allies of the nation. It appears, in fact, from the manner of his entertainment, that Sher Ali's object was to give the whole proceeding a national character. And the Russians in accepting this rôle have thrown down the gauntlet to us for supremacy in the frontier province of our own empire. Violating her repeated promises and engagements—which of course cannot be considered more binding than "the sacred word of honour of his Imperial Majesty the Tsar"—Russia has after long-continued and persevering efforts succeeded in gaining a footing in Afghanistan, and supplanting us there—in territory which is Indian and not Tatar; which is Khorassan and not Turkistan. Her presence and influence there can only mean mischief to us, and is not to be tolerated if we value our own position in India; especially after the very significant manner in which Sher Ali has welcomed his new allies, and emphasized his change of policy. The challenge thus thrown down by Russia has not quailed England, the British arms have crossed the frontier, and are now on Afghan soil. But before taking this decisive step the British Government, with that patience and forbearance which have throughout characterized its dealings with the Government of Afghanistan, sought to give the Amir a last chance of retrieving his false position.

As soon as the Government became aware of the actual lengths to which Sher Ali had gone in violation of his engagements, it resolved to send forthwith a counter-mission to Kabul, to demand explanations of the Amir; and the urgency of this measure was the greater by reason of the action taken by Russia in falsification of her solemn pledges to abstain from interference in the affairs of Afghanistan; whilst the object could be attained by no other means but a British Mission, because the Amir had adopted a course of reticence and estrangement which proscribed the resort to other agency of the same friendly nature. He not only closed his roads against us, but he steadily refused to answer the letters addressed to him by the Viceroy.

Accordingly, Nawab Ghulam Hasan Khan, C.S.I., a native gentleman, who had formerly resided at Kabul as British Agent at the court of the Amir, was sent forward to inform Sher Ali of the approach of a British Mission, and to request his good offices for its safe conduct and honourable treatment on the journey through his territories. He was also the bearer of a letter addressed by the Viceroy to Sher Ali. The reception of our messenger by the Amir, though not openly dishonourable, was by no means friendly, for he was placed under strict surveillance bordering upon imprisonment, and was allowed to make no communications to his own government that did not first pass through Sher Ali's hands and scrutiny. At this juncture, about the 17th July, Sardar Abdulla Jan, the favourite son and heir apparent of the Amir, died at Kabul of fever; and the event being made the most of for procrastination, the Government of India unhesitatingly postponed their business with the Amir till the expiry of the full period of forty days of mourning, and in the interim the Viceroy addressed a letter of condolence to Sher Ali upon his bereavement. The grief which left this letter unanswered, and deferred the attention to business on the side of India, was not so obstructive on the side of Turkistan, and messengers and letters passed to and fro in hot haste between Kabul and Tashkand without intermission. In this interval the arrangements of the Mission were completed, and the party assembled at Peshawar early in September in readiness to start. To give the Mission the best chances of success and the Amir every confidence in its friendliness, the Viceroy selected Sir Neville B. Chamberlain, an officer of high rank and distinction, who had long experience and intimate acquaintance with the Afghan people and country, and was besides a personal friend and acknowledged favourite of Sher Ali, for the chief command.

It was evident, however, on the arrival of the Mission at Peshawar that the Amir had not only made no arrangements for its reception, but, on the contrary, had taken very decisive measures to prevent its entering his territory. He had issued peremptory orders to the officers in command of his frontier outposts to close the road against us, should we attempt a passage, and to use force if necessary to prevent our passing the frontier. At the same time he strengthened his garrison at Ali Masjid with troops from Dhaka, and reinforced the army collected there with fresh troops from the capital. And finally, a day or two previous to the date fixed for the start of the Mission, he sent Mirakhir Ahmad Khan, Governor of Jalalabad, down to the Khybar outpost to see that our passage was effectually barred. Besides these manifest signs of Sher Ali's intentions, his commandant in the fort of Ali Masjid repeatedly and plainly informed the Peshawar authorities that his orders were positive to prevent the passage of the Mission, that he had been reprimanded for having given passage to Nawab Ghulam Hasan Khan, the Viceroy's messenger, and that if the Mission attempted to pass his post against orders and without a permit from the Amir, he had no alternative but to abide by his orders as a soldier, and to use force to prevent its passage.

Such being the state of affairs, and time passing away with no reply, or probability of a reply, coming from the Amir, it was decided that the Mission should advance to the Khybar and put to the test the assertions of the Amir's commandant at Ali Masjid. So, on the morning of the 20th September, the Mission marched from Peshawar to Jamrùd, at the entrance to the Khybar Pass, and camped there; whilst Major

Cavagnari, accompanied by Colonel Jenkins and Captain Wygram Battye, of the Corps of Guides, and twenty-four troopers of the regiment as escort, together with a small party of our own frontier village chiefs, and some representatives of the pass Afridis, rode on to Ali Masjid to see the commandant, and personally ascertain whether the road was open to the Mission or not. The commandant, Fyz Muhammad Khan, met Major Cavagnari and Colonel Jenkins (who with a few attendants advanced somewhat from the rest of their small party) at a spot a few hundred yards outside the fort, and in the course of the parley that ensued told them plainly what he had before communicated to the Peshawar Commissioner, namely, that his orders were to prevent the passage of the Mission, and that if it attempted to pass after this warning, he would be obliged to open fire upon it to turn it back. Fyz Muhammad also drew attention to the fact of Major Cavagnari being attended by a party of Afridi tribesmen, subjects of the Amir, and properly under his own command; censured him for seducing them from their allegiance, and said that, had he acted on strictly military principles, instead of on friendly motives, he would have been justified in firing upon the armed party approaching his fort in company with the Major. The refusal of a passage having been clearly established, and the conversation trenching upon delicate ground, amongst an audience continuously growing by fresh arrivals from the fort, Major Cavagnari skilfully brought the interview to a close, and both parties returned on their respective ways, Major Cavagnari and Fyz Muhammad shaking hands on departure as on meeting.

On the following day Sir N. Chamberlain returned to Peshawar with his camp, and the Mission was then and there dissolved, and the Viceroy's messenger recalled from Kabul. Thus came to a crisis the for years unsatisfactory, and of late unsafe, state of our relations with the Amir of Kabul. The rebuff of the Mission was decided, and the rejection of this last effort to adjust differences by friendly means premeditated. Sher Ali's act was meant to be insulting, and the insult was all the greater because it was unprovoked, and in the face of a long-enduring forbearance, such as no other great government would have had the courage to show. The conduct of Sher Ali throughout the course that has culminated in this final step of his beyond the pale of consideration from the British Government, is what was foreseen and predicted by those who have had opportunities of learning the Afghan character, and studying Afghan politics. The occasion is a good warning to us to trust no more to a broken reed. Sher Ali's conduct towards the British Government in this his defection from its alliance, and rejection of its friendship, is condemned by a very large portion of his own subjects, and by public opinion in India generally. It is the result of the instability and fickle ambition of the Afghan character, when let loose to its own devices, without the restraint of a paramount and guiding authority. It is the fruit of the exclusive policy initiated by Dost Muhammad and left by him as a legacy to his successors, whereby the country was hedged about with a wall of ignorance and prejudice, and kept stationary in its mediæval barbarism, whilst the rest of the world around it was advancing in the paths of civilization.

On the rejection of its friendly Mission by the Amir, the Government of India had no alternative but the resort to force. Orders were promptly issued for the assemblage of an army for service in the field, and it was expected that the Amir's insult would be at once avenged by the invasion of his territory. The British Government, however, averse to hasty action, resolved to give the Amir yet another opportunity of recovering his forfeited place in its friendship, and, accordingly the Government of India, postponing immediate action, addressed an ultimatum to Sher Ali, and granted him up to the 20th November for a satisfactory reply—the period of grace allowing ample time for an answer. The date fixed upon in due course came, but with it no reply. Sher Ali was obdurate, and obstinately maintained his silence. The order went forth, and on the morrow the British arms crossed the frontier into Afghan territory, and war against Sher Ali became an accomplished fact.

How and where the war now begun is destined to terminate, time will show. But it will be our own fault, if, with the opportunity now before us, we do not settle the question of our Indian frontier in this direction once and for all. It behoves us to remember, and the fact requires to be impressed upon our minds, that in our invasion of Afghanistan now, it is not the Amir of Kabul that we have to deal with alone, but with the fate and disposal of the entire territory over which we have recognized his rule, and which we have made for him what it is. But for our consistent aid and countenance, and very material support during the past thirty years, the rule and possessions of the Amir of Kabul would never have extended beyond the province of that name itself. The country would have remained a dismembered state held piecemeal by local native chiefs, eternally at feud with each other, and intriguing with foreigners for the maintenance of their several isolated positions. For the possession and retention of Kandahar, Herat, and Balkh the Amir Sher Ali Khan is indebted to the British Government; and it behoves us to take care that—either through the act of Sher Ali, or the interference of any other power —the solidarity of the Afghan possessions is not destroyed or damaged by our invasion.

We have now in entering Afghanistan to provide not only for its internal security and order, but we have also to provide for the safety of its frontiers against external aggression and intrigue. And the only way in which these objects of vital importance to the success of our enterprise, and of lasting benefit to the empire, can be attained with any prospect of a satisfactory and stable result, is by our taking their arrangement, execution, and control directly into our own hands. With British garrisons at Kabul, Kandahar, Herat, and Balkh—for which the existing army of India with but slight increment is amply sufficient in ordinary times—Afghanistan will be pacified, and Russia in the direction of Persia and Bukhara be deprived of an object of ambition and field of intrigue.

Afghanistan thus secured, her people around these centres of protection will devote themselves to industry and the profits of a for long untilled soil. And prosperity radiating will soon spread over the country to the development of its rich treasures and internal resources, and to the speedy creation of a real bulwark of the British Empire in India. Of the realization of this picture we have solid grounds of hope in the brilliant results of the experiment of British rule over the million of our Afghan subjects on the Trans-Indus frontier. And that, too, under the disadvantageous circumstances of their contact with the independent and lawless hill-tribes, who are free from the pressure and control of any government or fixed authority behind them.

Leaving alone the discussion of the military and political aspects of our occupation of Afghanistan as questions for the consideration and settlement of governments, let us inquire who the people of Afghanistan are, and see what are their affinities and relations with the people of Hindustan.

The Afghan nation, as understood by us, comprises all the inhabitants proper of Afghanistan. And this leads to the inquiry—What is Afghanistan? Literally, the word means "place or country of the Afghan," as Hindustan does of the Hindu, and Turkistan of the Turk, &c. But it is not a geographical term in the same sense as the examples mentioned. Nor is it the name used by the Afghans themselves to designate their country. The term appears to have come into prominent use only in modern times, to designate the territory in which the Afghan is the dominant race—just as Balochistan signifies the territory of the Baloch. Both at the same time being divisions of an extensive geographical area known by the name of Khorassan. And this is the term used by both Afghan and Baloch to designate their native country—the terms Afghanistan and Balochistan being employed only by foreigners.

The word Khorassan itself is said to be a mere euphonism of Khoristan or "the country of the sun," "the place of light." Or, in other words, "the East," "the Orient," as being the easternmost or Indian province of the ancient Persian Empire—of the empire of Cyrus and Darius. The terminal word *stàn* or *istàn* means, when affixed in combination with another word, "the place where a thing abounds," as *kohistàn*, "the place of hills, highlands," or *gulistàn*, "the place of flowers, a garden," or *nayistàn*, "the place of reeds, a reedy swamp," or *inglistàn*, "England, the country of the English," and so on.

Amongst themselves, however, the Afghans more commonly speak of their country as Pukhtùn-khwà, "Pathàn country," or Watan-khwà, "Home country"—the terminal word in their own language signifying "side, quarter, tract, coast." But these terms carry with them the precise definition of the country actually peopled by the Pukhtùn themselves, in distinction to the territory peopled by foreign tribes amongst them or connected with them, as Kafiristan by the Kafir, and Hazàrajàt by the Hazara, &c., within the integral area of Khorassan.

Again, the term Khorassan is used to designate a well-known geographical area, as well as a distinct portion of it, just as the word England is used to designate the whole island as well as a distinct portion of it. The limits of the whole area are held to be the Indus river on the east, and the desert of Yazd on the west; the river Oxus (in its ancient course) on the north, and the Arabian sea on the south. That is to say, Khorassan is bounded on the east by Hindustan or India, and on the west by Iràn or Persia; on the north by Turàn or Turkistan—which was called by the Arab conquerors Màwarànahar, "beyond the river," or Transoxiana—and on the south by the sea. The lesser portion of this region—designated by the same name as the whole—is a narrow strip of highland country which lies north and south along its western coasts. It is generally distinguished as Irani Khorassan on account of its long possession—in the modern age, only interrupted by the short-lived conquest of the Durrani—by the Persians, who, indeed, in the thirteenth century held the whole region down to the Indus. How they came to lose this territory we need not here delay to inquire; but we may note that their hold of it appears to have been finally shaken by the invasion of Changiz Khan during the first half of that century. In fact, this Mongol conqueror, like his predecessor Sabaktakin the Turk, in his devastating course over the country, produced a very considerable dislocation of the population, and left a powerful colony of his countrymen firmly planted in the stronghold of the territory, where they are to this day, as we shall see farther on. Changiz at the time of his invasion found the Peshawar valley held by Irac or Persian troops, and the adjoining valley of Swat—which was then called Swati Gabri, or Swat of the Gabr—a stronghold of the Fire-worshippers. That the Persians dominated this region for long after the catastrophe of the Mongol invasion is certain, for under their recovered sway the Mongol colony forgot its mother tongue and learned the Persian. At this period, and onwards up to the time of the Mughal conquest under Babur, the language of Khorassan was Persian, the Pukhto and other dialects being confined to the hill-regions and inaccessible corners of the country.

The limits of Irani Khorassan are not well defined, and would appear to be more of a political than of a tribal or geographical character. The country generally may be said to comprise the succession of elevated valleys and plateaux which echelon the range of hills extending from Mashhad in the north to Korian in the south, together with the strip of country skirting its base on either side. In fact, if it had not remained a possession of Persia, the distinction of name would not have arisen, and the territory would have formed part of the province or country of Hari, to which it properly belongs. It is, however, separated from Herat by a belt of desert and sand which extends north and south between Khaf and

Sistan. As it is, this region forms a buttress of hills on the west side of Khorassan corresponding with that on the east side formed by the range of the Suleman mountains—the two being connected towards the north by the cross range of the Hindu Kush and its western prolongations.

These three mountain barriers, with their *kohdàman*, or "mountain skirt," along the outer base of each, form the true boundaries of Khorassan—boundaries which, as before mentioned, are the Indus on the east, the Oxus in the line of its ancient course on the north, and the desert of Yazd on the west. The region thus defined is the Khorassan of the ancient Persian Empire—its province of India—and up to the time of the Arab conquest in the eighth century of our era

Persian was the common language of the country, and the Persian was its dominant people. The language is still spoken, and with but comparatively little change, in several parts of the country inhabited by the representatives of its ancient rulers—as in Sistan and Makran towards the south-west, and in Ghorband and Badakhshan towards the north-east, as well as in many parts of the interior of Balochistan and Afghanistan, where the Parsiwan and the Tàjik are found at the present day. And it is the language of the Hazàra Mongols in Ghor.

Khorassan, then, is the region buttressed against Iran on the west, and Hindustan on the east, and Turkistan on the north by great mountain ranges, the two first of which abut upon the Arabian sea towards the south—in which direction they are connected by a cross-line of bold cliffs and sea coast. The whole region is mountainous and elevated, and presents a very diversified aspect, so far as concerns its physical configuration. And the remarkable feature of this region is that its interior has no river that reaches the sea. The mountains in the north are more or less clothed with forests; in the south they are bare; whilst in both directions the valleys are fertile and watered by perennial streams. The central region spreads out into wide plains or steppes, and these are coursed by rivers which concentrate in the south-west of the area, where the space is occupied by a vast desert of moving sands. As may be naturally understood, the valleys in the north and south are the principal centres of population—they are, apart from the cities, the sites where the population is densest.

The climate of the region is as diversified as its surface, the seasons being largely affected by the natural configuration of the land. Spring and summer, which are delightful seasons and mild or temperate in the sheltered valleys and on the elevated plateaux, are tryingly hot and arid, or intolerably scorching on the steppes and borders of the desert, and amongst the bare rocky hills of the south. The autumn and winter, which in the sheltered valleys of the north are severe only from the hardships of snow, are rigorous on the elevated plateaux of the south and the wide steppes of the central region from the blighting effects of keen winds and biting frosts. In the north the people are fair or rufous, in the south they are dusky or black.

Considered from a national as well as

political point of view, Khorassan comprises two great countries with many points of resemblance, few of divergence—they are Balochistan and Afghanistan. The distinction between the two is of modern date and more of a political nature, the ancient polity having been one and the same for both. In fact, the Afghan and Baloch consider each other of allied race—as brethren descended from a common stock. Balochistan is the smaller country of the two, and occupies only the southern portion of the whole region.

In the time of the ancient sovereignty of India its people were Budhist, and in that of Persia they were Magian (Magh, Gabr) as to religion. Relics of both these religions are still extant in the country. Of the first in the *cheda* or "funeral pillars," which are still erected by the Brahoe nomads, as well as in the wedding-rings formed by them of stones set in circles on their pasture-grounds (see my "Indus to the Tigris:" Trübner and Co.). The funeral pillars, though the fact is unknown to the people of the present day, who are professedly—and very much more so than practically—Musalman, are the representatives of the Budhist *chaitiya* or *chorten*, which is still in full force in the Budhist countries of Nepal and Ladak, and is to be traced amongst the Afghans and Pathans in the *tsalai*, or the heap of stones piled over the graves of their saints and religious martyrs. The wedding-rings, on the other hand, are emblems of the *yunilingam* type adopted from the Brahmin, whose religion supplanted that of Buddha. And of the other in the *gabr* or *gaur-band* or *gaur-basta* —the stone platforms of the *àtash-kada* or "fire temple." The term *gaurband* or *gaurbasta* of itself gives no clue to the real object and nature of these structures. The meaning conveyed by the term is simply something "made or built up by the Gabr," and is evidently one employed by foreigners. Probably the name was first applied to these relics of the Fire-worshippers by the early Arab conquerors, who swept them and theirs clean out of the country, or else by their successors, who, as Musalmans and iconoclasts, cared nothing for the antiquities of the pagan and the infidel. However, putting aside the consideration of Balochistan and its people—the subject, full of interest as it is, not being immediately connected with the purpose of our present inquiry—let us confine our attention to Afghanistan and the Afghan people.

By Afghanistan is meant the northern division of the Korassan country previously defined. Its southern limits, from the river Indus, westward are along the line of the valleys of Sibi, Peshin, and Sho-rawak to the desert of Sistan, and that province itself. The country is divided into numerous districts, many of which retain ancient names, the origin and signification of which are subjects inviting investigation, whilst others are named after the tribes now occupying them. But besides these, there are several large divisions of the territory which constitute distinct countries or provinces with marked differences between them. The principal of these are Roh and Kabul, Zabul and Sistan, Hari and Ghor, and Balkh and Badakhshan. The limits of none of them are very clearly defined, and as employed at the present day the several terms are used very loosely in the coupled connexion above given. Thus Roh and Kabul are often spoken of as one and the same country, yet there are parts of Roh which are not Kabul, and there are parts of Kabul which are not Roh. And this, apart altogether from the political sense in which the name Kabul is used (from the fact of its being the recognized seat of government) to designate the entire territory of the kingdom or khanate. And so it is with Zabul and Sistan, the latter being spoken of as Zabul, but all Zabul not being Sistan. In other words, Kabul and Zabul, or Kabulistan and Zabulistan, are two great divisions of country: one of which contains Roh and the other Sistan. It is to some extent the same with Hari and Ghor, and to a lesser extent also with the

Balkh and Badakhshan provinces. Still, notwithstanding this loose application of the names, there is a distinction between the several countries to which they properly belong, and I propose to consider each separately in as brief terms as possible.

Roh is said to have the same signification as Koh, which means "Mountain," and includes all the country of the Suleman range and Khybar hills, as far as it is occupied by Pathans. That is to say, from Bajaur and Boner in the north, to Sibi and Peshin in the south; and from the river Indus on the east, to Ghazni and the Khwaja Amran range on the west. The people of this country call themselves Rohilai, and are known in India as Rohilla. In Persia and western countries they are more generally styled Sulemani, a term which is familiar to the people of the central part of the region only. In English the terms Roh and Rohilai are correctly rendered by "Highlands" and "Highlander." During the successive invasions of India by Mahmùd of Ghazni in the tenth century whole tribes of these hill-people, with their families and flocks, accompanied his armies as military colonists, and settled in different parts of the conquered territory; notably in the district to the north of Oude, which is named after them Rohilkand—a district which there are grounds for believing was the home of their remote ancestors. These Highlanders are a very martial people, and addicted to soldiering. Large numbers of them are to be found in the ranks of our Native army, and amongst the forces maintained by our feudatory princes and chiefs.

Kabul is the name of the country between Ghazni and Sufed Koh, on the south, and the Hindu Kush on the north. The Lohgar valley is its southern district, and the Pughmàn hills on the Hazara border of Ghor form its western boundary. The eastern limit is defined by the Kunar river and Chitral valley; though by some it is held to extend to the Indus from the junction of the Kabul river northwards to the vicinity of Gilgit. But for this extension there is no justification, the whole of the tract between the Kunar or Chitral river, and this portion of the Indus, being independent territory, and called Yàghistàn or "unconquered country." The northern part of Kabul up to the watershed of Hindu Kush is called Kohistan or "Highlands," and that part of it on the southern slopes of Hindu Kush is distinguished as

Kafiristan, or the "Kafir country," the country of the Pagans or Infidels—it is altogether independent. Kafiristan, as will be gathered from its meaning, is not a geographical term. In the early centuries of the establishment of Islam in these regions the term was applied to a very extensive area held by peoples who refused the new religion, and it included all the inaccessible country on both sides of the Hindu Kush and the Himalaya, as far as Little Tibet or Ladak. Both Badakhshan and Baltistan were included in Kafiristan as late as the middle of the sixteenth century, when Babur founded the Mughal Empire in India. All Yaghistan, with Swat and Boner, were at the same period included in Kafiristan. All these countries are now professedly Musalman, and the term Kafiristan at the present day is limited to a very restricted and gradually diminishing area on the southern slopes of Hindu Kush, directly to the north of Kabul. All the converted portion of the former Kafiristan to the south of the Himalaya and Hindu Kush, as far as the Pathan limits in Bajaur and Boner, is called collectively Kohistan.

Zabul is the old name of the country to the south of Kabul, and is not now in general use, though well known to the people, the modern term Kandahar having superseded it, except perhaps in books. It includes all the country from Ghazni westward to the river Helmand as far as Bust or Bost (now in ruins), together with the country about the sources of that river, or drained by its upper course. It is a very extensive region, but is not so densely peopled as is Kabul. Its southern limit is

Peshin, and its eastern the range of the Kach Tobah hills, which connects the Khwaja Amran with the western offshoots from the Sufed Koh to the south of Ghazni. Ghazni itself forms the north-eastern limit, whilst the northern is formed by the Siyah Koh range of Ghor. This division is not well watered, and is more open than any other part of the country except Sistan, with which it is continuous.

Sistan, formerly called Sijistan, and known also by the name of Nimroz, is the country which fills the south-west corner of Afghanistan up to the Helmand, between Bust and Girishk; though by some it is held to extend up to the vicinity of Ghazni—in fact, to include all the country drained by the Helmand. In former times it was a very flourishing province of Persia, but was finally depopulated and ruined by Nadir; and after his death it was incorporated with the Durrani Empire, until partitioned by the Arbitration of 1872. The country, especially Sistan proper—the basin of the Helmand—has never recovered its former prosperity, and is now very thinly peopled by a remnant of the ancient possessors, mixed up with outlaws and castaways from the neighbouring countries, and encroached upon by Afghan and Baloch colonists. The Persians, however, who have now recovered the best part of the region, are gradually restoring it from its long neglect and decay; and if they possessed the energy and enterprise of Europeans, would soon make it a very valuable acquisition.

Hari is the country of Herat, the ancient Aria, and lies to the north of

Sistan. It forms the western province of Khorassan, and was incorporated with Afghanistan by the founder of the Durrani Empire. It has been maintained ever since as part of the kingdom, though shorn of its outlying districts of Ghani, Birjand, Záwah, &c., up to Kochan and Chinaran during the reign of his successor. It is a fertile country, and important as the key of Afghanistan from the west and north. It forms a mountain barrier for Afghanistan on the west, as Roh does on the east. Its people are called Haravi or Herati, and consist of Parsiwans, Tajiks, and Hazara Mongols. Its political boundary on the side of Persia is the strip of desert which extends from Sistan to Khaff, and thence the line of the Hari Rud, or Herat river, to the vicinity of Sarakhs. Its southern limit is the district of Sabzwar, and the northern the Turkman desert, whilst to east it extends to the skirt of the Ghor hills and the Murghab river.

Ghor is the mountainous country—as its name signifies—which is situated between Herat and Kabul in one direction, and Kandahar and Balkh in the other. It is formed by the western prolongations of Hindu Kush, and is peopled by a number of Mongol tribes who were settled here as military colonists by Changiz Khan—as Rohilkand was colonized with Rohillas by Mahmùd of Ghazni—after the expulsion and extermination of the original Persian possessors. Its people are collectively styled Hazara by the Afghans, and it is the term by which they speak of themselves. The term is also employed to designate their country. In both cases on account of the original military disposition of the colony. In Persian Hazara means a division or disposition by thousands, and in its application here is the equivalent of the Tatar term *tuman*, or camp, or military division. The region is watered by the sources and upper courses of the Herat and Murghab rivers, and very little is known about it; for though included in Afghanistan, it is entirely independent as regards its interior districts, whilst its outskirts in the direction of Kabul, Kandahar, Herat, and Balkh only pay revenue on pressure. Its people are Shia' Musalmans of the Ali Ilahi sect, who believe in the divinity of Ali.

Balkh is the strip of country between the northern base of Hindu Kush and its western prolongation, and the river Oxus as far as Khwaja Salih, and thence across an arid desert to the Sarakhs frontier. By some this part of the line is held to be along the course of the ancient bed of the river. The western limit is at the Murghab river, and the eastern at Cunduz. It is an important frontier province, as it commands Herat on one side, and Kabul on the other. It is now in a very neglected and unsettled state, but under a secure and good government is capable of much development. At present the territory is divided amongst a number of different races, mostly Tajik and Mongol, with some Uzbak and Turk colonists from the other side of the river, and a few camps of nomade Turkmans. All are subjects of the Afghan, and as a rule very turbulent ones, there being very few, if any, Afghan tribes settled amongst them, and only a small garrison of the Kabul army at Tashkurghan. The province was first incorporated with the Durrani Empire by Ahmad Shah, was lost in the reign of his successor, and finally recovered to the kingdom by the Amir Dost Muhammad Khan in 1850.

Badakhshan is the country in the north-east corner of Afghanistan, and comprises all the territory drained by the sources of the Oxus as far west as the Wakhsh river, beyond which lie the Turk districts of Caratakin and Hissar. It is a poor and mountainous country throughout, and comprises the plain of Fyzabad with the tributary valleys of Darwaz, Roshan, Shughuan, and Wakhan. It has only in part been recently added to the Afghan dominions—to which it had been lost (except as a nominal tributary to the Amir Dost Muhammad Khan) since the death of Ahmad Shah, Durrani—through the good offices of the British Government, and the political frontier is now at the Panja river. The rest of the country is independent, but is fast passing under Russian influence for want of consideration and support on the side of Kabul or India. Its hidden mineral wealth is entirely unexplored, and the mines of ruby and turquoise, for which the region has long been celebrated, are altogether neglected and undeveloped. Iron of excellent quality is also found in this country. Its people are pure Arians of the ancient Persian stock, with many Tajiks amongst them.

Such must here suffice for our very brief enumeration of the principal countries included within the limits of Afghanistan. Let us now note who are the people inhabiting and possessing them. And this we will do in the briefest manner compatible with the fair comprehension of the subject, for to treat each case fully would easily fill volumes—volumes too of very interesting matter.

As before mentioned, the term Afghan is commonly employed by us to designate the inhabitants of Afghanistan collectively. The term, however, strictly speaking, is applicable only to one section of the people, and that by no means the most numerous in the country. The people of Afghanistan, in fact, are not a mixed race in the sense of miscegenation; on the contrary, they are a conglomeration of several distinct nationalities which do not intermarry, and each of which maintains its own traditions, and customs, and dialects, more or less completely distinct from the others. The Afghan is merely the dominant race amongst them, and, though figuring prominently in the history of the country from a very early period—and more especially since the introduction of Islam by Mahmùd of Ghazni—has only attained its present independence and position of dominance since the middle of last century.

The Afghans claim an Israelitish descent (see my "Journal of a Mission to Kandahar in 1857-8," Smith, Elder, and Co., London), and call themselves "Bani Israil." They are proud of and lay great stress on this title, and consider themselves a peculiar people, distinct from those amongst whom they are now settled. Yet they call themselves Pukhtùn in common with the rest of the Pukhto-speaking tribes. But they are careful to make the difference, and excluding other Pukhtùns from their genealogies, do not admit that they are true Afghans. In other words, all

Afghans are Pukhtùns, but all the Pukhtùns are not Afghans. From this it would appear that a national language is the bond of connexion. According to their own accounts, they were originally carried away into captivity from Palestine to Media by Nebuchadnezzar. Subsequently they emigrated to Ghor; and thence they finally spread over the country to their present locations. The nation, as it exists to-day, traces its descent from a common ancestor named Kais or Kish, through three great branches named Batan, Ghurghusht, and Saraband, or Sarabaur. This Kais, they say, was one of the early disciples of Muhammad, and converted his people to the new faith promulgated by the Arabian prophet. The prophet changed his name to 'Abdurrashid —"the servant of the Guide" (God)—and as he was to be the master-guide of his people in the way they should go, he gave him the title of "Pahtan," which is said to signify "rudder" in the Syrian language. Of the three great tribes said to be descended from this apostle of Islam, the first is said to have emigrated to Hindustan, and there become lost amongst its people; the second—which appears to have derived its name from its location in Ghor—also largely emigrated to India; whilst the third—which appears to be named after its real Indian parentage, Sarabaur, being the Pukhto form of Suryabans, "the Solar race," the Rajput of Hindustan—remained in their native seats. In this traditionary account, it will be noticed, no provision is made for the disposal of the other Afghans cotemporary with Kais. Nor have the Afghans at this time any knowledge of their fate or whereabouts. Now, though distinguishing themselves from other Pukhtùns in lineage, the Afghan in no respect differs from them in language or polity, both alike being bound by the Pukhtùn code or "Pukhtùnwali"—an unwritten law, which, though somewhat modified by the ordinances of Islam, is very similar in character and principle to that given by Moses to the Hebrews; and it has besides so many points of resemblance to the Rajput customs as to raise the suspicion of a real connexion. It is possible that the Afghan really may be an Israelite, as he asserts, who has become absorbed into Rajput tribes; for whole colonies of the latter people are known by the records of history to have moved into Afghanistan with the Pandu kings after their defeat in the great contest on the field of Kurukshetr, "the field of the Kuru" near Thanesar, north of Delhi—the Mahabharat fought between the Suryabans and the Chandrabans, the Solar race and the Lunar race, for sovereignty in India at the dawn of Indian history. Whatever his origin, however, the Afghan is now, and has been for ages, completely identified as an Indian. The Afghans—or Durranis, as they have since their independence as a nation styled themselves,—are now settled principally in the Kandahar country, and especially in the valleys drained by the sources of the Helmand river—a region which may be considered as their real home. From it they extend westwards into the border districts of Sistan and Herat as Popalzai and Alikozai; to the eastward they extend as far as the Tobah hills, which are held by the Achakzai and Saddozai; to the north-eastward they spread into Kabul as Barakzai; and thence through the ancient Gandaria, held by the Mahmandzai or Mohmands, to Bajaur, Swat, and Buner (the Greek Massagaur) and the adjoining portion of the Peshawar valley as the Yusufzai. In Kabul and Kandahar they share the soil with other peoples, but in the hill-tracts and Peshawar they possess the land entirely.

Next to the Afghan as the dominant people comes the Pukhtùn as the national people. The Pukhtùn or Pathan, as distinct from the Afghan, is located altogether on the eastern coasts of the country—on the Suleman range and its offshoots—and includes a great variety of tribes who are only bound together by a common language and code, and in other respects are more or less antagonistic, with rival interests and avoidance of intermarriage. In India this people is known by the name of Pathan, which is merely the Hindustani form of Pukhtàna—the plural of Pukhtùn—whatever be the value of the native tradition as to the Syrian title bestowed by the Arabian Prophet on his apostle to the Afghans.

According to the current idea the term Pukhtùn—plural Pukhtàna—means a "Highlander," and Pukhto or Pushto "the language of the Highlanders," and the derivation is thus explained. Pukhta or Pushta—the former harsh form is used in the east, and the latter soft form in the west of the country—means a "hill" or "bank," or "elevated land;" Pukhtun or Pushtun the inhabitant of that land; and Pukhto or Pushto the language spoken by him. This looks simple enough, but there are certain important facts which militate against its validity. In the first place, the term Pukhtùn is not by Pathans themselves—though it is by strangers—applied to all the inhabitants of the highlands occupied by that people, nor to all those who, dwelling amongst them, use that language and that only. On the contrary, foreigners—settled for ages amongst them—are carefully debarred the title of Pukhtùn by its proper owners, and are severally distinguished according to their origin as Hindki, Gujar, Tajik, Turk, Uzbak, Hindu, Jat, &c., as the case may be; and these foreigners themselves severally never claim the title of Pukhtùn, except perhaps when they come down to lower India and adopt the term to indicate whence they come. Pukhtùn, then, is a distinct national title, and Pukhtùn-khwa the name of the country inhabited by the Pukhtùn, and Pukhto the language spoken by that people. It is probable that the terms are identical with the Pactyi and Pactyea of Herodotus. In the mouth of an Afridi of the Khybar the pronunciation favours the latter view—apart altogether from other considerations—for he calls himself Pakhtun, and his language Pakhto.

Of the several tribes reckoned as Pukhtùn or Pathàn several are evidently of Indian origin, judging from their names, such as the Khatrini (Khatri or Hindu military caste), Sheorani (Shiva sect of Hindus), Kakar (Gakar tribe of Indians in the north Panjab), Tori (Tuari tribe of Rajputs), &c. All these Pathan tribes are located on the Suleman and Khybar ranges from the Kabul river in the north to the Kaura or

Vahou Pass in the south. This pass debouches on the Indus riverain opposite Dera Fatah Khan, in the middle of the Derajat, and marks the boundary between the Pathan and the Baloch. All to the southward of this is held by the Baloch, except a small tract held by the Khatranis, who are here isolated amongst the Baloch. As before mentioned, the Pathans of this region are sometimes called Sulemani, after the range of hills they inhabit, but generally the term is restricted to the tribes in the centre of the range. Some of the tribes, as the Waziris, Lohanis, Kakars, Ghilzais, &c., are also known by the name Povindia or Parwindia, a term—derived from the Persian *parwinda*, a "bale of merchandise,"—which signifies their occupation as "packmen," "mercantile travellers," &c., for they are the people who drive the caravans to and fro between Khorassan and Hindustan, and monopolize the whole carrying trade of the country.

Connected with the Afghan and generally reckoned as a Pathan is the Ghilzai. His language is the Pukhto, and his manners and customs assimilate to those of the Afghan, with whom he is an orthodox Sunni Musalman. But he is professedly of a different origin, and never styles himself anything but Ghilji. He has no knowledge why he sticks to this term as his patronymic, beyond the fact that he is not an Afghan nor a Pathan, though now he is more or less blended with them by intermixture of territory, and to a small extent by intermarriage also. The Ghilzais are supposed to have come into the country with Sabaktakin the Turk in the tenth century, and to be representatives of the

Turk tribe of Khilich which was anciently located on the upper course of the Jaxartes. They are a very numerous and powerful tribe, and extend from the west side of the Khybar to Kabul, and thence across the western emanations of the Sufed Koh to Ghazni, and onwards down the Tarnak valley to Kandahar and Peshin, in which latter localities their chief tribes are the Hotak, Tokhi, and Tarin. Their chiefs take a leading part in the politics of the country, and since the accession of the Barakzai to power, have always exercised considerable influence at the court of Kabul. Unlike the rest of their fellow-countrymen, they are said to be generally hostile to the British and friendly to the Russian. They are a pre-eminently martial race, and only short of exercising the sovereignty, are quite as influential in

Afghanistan as the Afghan. A large portion of the tribe is still nomadic in its habits. Those in Kabul spend the summer on the uplands of Sufed Koh and winter in Gardez, Zurmat, and the country south of Ghazni to Abistada. Those in Kandahar summer in the Tobah range and Khwaja Amran, and winter on the borders of the desert of Sistan along the south bank of the Tarnak river down to its junction with the Helmand. This mode of life, necessitating a change from the high to the low lands with the seasons, is the cause of their subjection to the government, for without their winter quarters on the plain country they could not exist themselves, or their flocks.

Another principal people of Afghanistan is the Tajik or Tazik. The term means Arabian, and is applied to anything of

Arab origin produced or reared out of Arabia, and especially in Persia. For example, an imported Arab horse or dog, &c., is called Arabi, but one reared abroad from imported Arab stock is called Tàzi. So Arabs who emigrated with their families from Arabia and settled abroad are called Arab (or Sayyid, if connected with the family of Ali), and their full-bred offspring also are called by the same name. But the offspring and descendants of Arabs who married women of the country in which they settled are called Tazik or Tajik. In Afghanistan the term is applied collectively to all the people of ancient Persian origin who speak their mother-tongue, and includes Parsiwans, or pure Persians, with the Dihcan, or Dihgan, or Dihwar, who is of Arab descent by a native mother, and also the ancient Persian inhabitants of

Badakhshan and Sistan. The Tajik is everywhere devoted to the cultivation of the soil, and in the towns and cities carries on most of the mercantile business of the country, as well as providing the handicraftsmen and scribes for all the usual pursuits and trades of domestic industry—neither the Afghan or other Pathan engaging in any occupation but that of the farmer, the soldier, and the merchant. In fact, throughout the country to the west of the Suleman range — where he is principally found—the Tajik is the servant of the Pathan; and his place on the east of the range is filled by the Hindki.

The Hindki, like the Tajik on the other side of the Suleman range, is the descendant of Arab settlers, or of early Musalman converts, by Hindustani or Indian mothers.

He is confined almost entirely to the Indus provinces of Afghanistan.

Next to the Tajik—and like him speaking a dialect of Persian—is the Mongol located in Ghor or Hazara. This people are the descendants of the military colonists settled in this region by Changiz Khan, when he subjugated Afghanistan, intent on the conquest of India. Though they have, with the exception of a few domestic terms, entirely lost their native language, they have retained the physical and physiognomic characters of their race in perfect integrity, and they are as pure Mongols now as when they first settled here six hundred years ago. This is explained by the isolation of their position, and the peculiar system of Changiz Khan's conquests, to which he moved his hordes with their families and flocks and worldly goods, as well as to the thorough manner in which they swept Ghor clear of its ancient inhabitants. As before stated, they are known to the Afghans by the term Hazara, and this is the name by which they call themselves, outside their own limits at all events. They comprise numerous divisions or camps all styled Hazara, and distinguished by the addition of the tribal name, as Hazara Jaghuri, Hazara Carabaghi, Hazara Besudi, Hazara Dih Zangi, Hazara Jamshedi, Hazara Char Aymaghi, Hazara Tymani, &c., &c. To the north, towards the Oxus, they come in contact with the mixed population of Balkh—with the Tajik and Usbak, the Turk and Turkman, but without mixing with either. In fact, they intermarry with none of the races around them, and in the interior of their territory are entirely independent.

Finally, to the north of Kabul are the Kohistani people, or "people of the hill-country." They are composed of the ancient Persians and the ancient Indians. The former as far eastward as the Alishang river; the other onwards thence into Kashmir. The former speak Persian, and are all subjects of the Kabul Government; the other speak a variety of different dialects, which are unintelligible to their neighbours in adjoining glens even—though, with one or two exceptions, they are all of cognate stock with the Sanscrit. These ancient Indians are divided into numerous small communities or tribes, having little intercourse with the world around them, and eternally at war with each other. They are collectively styled Kohistani, but are distinguished as Kafir or "Infidel," Musalman or "Muhammadan," and Nimcha or "Half-and-half,"—that is to say, a new convert or the offspring of a Musalman by a Kafir woman. These people in all the country northward of Chaghan Sarae up to Hindu Kush, and as far as the Kashmir border in Yasin are independent. Whilst Badakhshan and Wakhan on the other side of the range are Kabul subjects.

The foregoing brief account of Afghanistan and the Afghans, will, it is trusted, enable the reader to form a clear idea of the past and present of the country and its people. At the same time it will serve to explain how it is that the country has never been able to maintain itself in any degree of security or prosperity as an independent kingdom without the support derived from external sources of aid—either by military expeditions, as in the time of the Saddozai, or else by diplomatic negotiations as in the time of the Barakzai. It will show how the progress of time has altered both the political situation and the popular sentiment of the country, and brought it back into closer relations with and fuller dependence upon the paramount power which has succeeded and taken the place of the great Empire of which it formerly constituted the frontier province towards Persia and Turkistan. Finally, it will illustrate the error of trusting—without adequate guarantee, as we have done—the safety and peace of the Empire to the hands of a barbarous and untrustworthy neighbour, who claims all manner of support and assistance as the guardian of its most important frontiers, and yet scorns control and the free communication absolutely necessary under the altered circumstances of his position, not only to the prosperity of his own kingdom, but to the well-being of the paramount Empire, and who holds himself at liberty to dispose of his country and his power for or against the Empire to which he owes his very existence, as it may seem to suit his own fancy or ambition—forgetful alike of past favours, and the value of the friendship he has rejected.

THE END.

A Catalogue of American and Foreign Books Published or Imported by MESSRS. SAMPSON LOW & CO. *can be had on application.*

Crown Buildings, 188, *Fleet Street, London,*
October, 1878.

A List of Books

PUBLISHED BY

SAMPSON LOW, MARSTON, SEARLE, & RIVINGTON.

ALPHABETICAL LIST.

A CLASSIFIED Educational Catalogue of Works published in Great Britain. Demy 8vo, cloth extra. Second Edition, revised and corrected to Christmas, 1877, 5*s*.

Abney (Captain W. de W., R.E., F.R.S.) Thebes, and its Five Greater Temples. Forty large Permanent Photographs, with descriptive letter-press. Super-royal 4to, cloth extra, 63*s*.

About Some Fellows. By an ETON BOY, Author of "A Day of my Life." Cloth limp, square 16mo, 2*s*. 6*d*.

Adventures of Captain Mago. A Phœnician's Explorations 1000 years B.C. By LEON CAHUN. Numerous Illustrations. Crown 8vo, cloth extra, gilt, 7*s*. 6*d*.

Adventures of a Young Naturalist. By LUCIEN BIART, with 117 beautiful Illustrations on Wood. Edited and adapted by PARKER GILLMORE. Post 8vo, cloth extra, gilt edges, New Edition, 7*s*. 6*d*.

Adventures in New Guinea. The Narrative of the Captivity of a French Sailor for Nine Years among the Savages in the Interior. Small post 8vo, with Illustrations and Map, cloth, gilt, 6*s*.

Africa, and the Brussels Geographical Conference. Translated from the French of EMILE BANNING, by R. H. MAJOR, F.S.A. With Map, crown 8vo, 7*s*. 6*d*.

Alcott (Louisa M.) Aunt Jo's Scrap-Bag. Square 16mo, 2*s*. 6*d*. (Rose Library, 1*s*.)

—— *Cupid and Chow-Chow.* Small post 8vo, 3*s*. 6*d*.

—— *Little Men: Life at Plumfield with Jo's Boys.* Small post 8vo, cloth, gilt edges, 3*s*. 6*d*. (Rose Library, Double vol. 2*s*.)

—— *Little Women.* 1 vol., cloth, gilt edges, 3*s*. 6*d*. (Rose Library, 2 vols., 1*s*. each.)

Alcott (Louisa M.) Old-Fashioned Girl. Best Edition, small post 8vo, cloth extra, gilt edges, 3*s.* 6*d.* (Rose Library, 2*s.*)

—— *Work and Beginning Again.* A Story of Experience. 1 vol., small post 8vo, cloth extra, 6*s.* Several Illustrations. (Rose Library, 2 vols., 1*s.* each.)

—— *Shawl Straps.* Small post 8vo, cloth extra, gilt, 3*s.* 6*d.*

—— *Eight Cousins; or, the Aunt Hill.* Small post 8vo, with Illustrations, 3*s.* 6*d.*

—— *The Rose in Bloom.* Small post 8vo. cloth extra, 3*s.* 6*d.*

—— *Silver Pitchers.* Small post 8vo, cloth extra, 3*s.* 6*d.*

—— *Under the Lilacs.* Small post 8vo, cloth extra, 5*s.*

"Miss Alcott's stories are thoroughly healthy, full of racy fun and humour . . . exceedingly entertaining . . . . We can recommend the 'Eight Cousins.'"—*Athenæum.*

Alpine Ascents and Adventures; or, Rock and Snow Sketches. By H. SCHÜTZ WILSON, of the Alpine Club. With Illustrations by WHYMPER and MARCUS STONE. Crown 8vo, 10*s.* 6*d.* 2nd Edition.

Andersen (Hans Christian) Fairy Tales. With Illustrations in Colours by E. V. B. Royal 4to, cloth, 25*s.*

Andrews (Dr.) Latin-English Lexicon. 14th Edition. Royal 8vo, 1670 pp., cloth extra, price 18*s.*

Anecdotes of the Queen and Royal Family. Collected and Edited by J. G. HODGINS, with Illustrations. New Edition, 5*s.*

Animals Painted by Themselves. Adapted from the French of Balzac, Georges Sands, &c., with 200 Illustrations by GRANDVILLE. 8vo, cloth extra, gilt, 10*s.* 6*d.*

Art of Reading Aloud (The) in Pulpit, Lecture Room, or Private Reunions, with a perfect system of Economy of Lung Power on just principles for acquiring ease in Delivery, and a thorough command of the Voice. By G. VANDENHOFF, M.A. Crown 8vo, cloth extra, 6*s.*

Asiatic Turkey: being a Narrative of a Journey from Bombay to the Bosphorus, embracing a ride of over One Thousand Miles, from the head of the Persian Gulf to Antioch on the Mediterranean. By GRATTAN GEARY, Editor of the *Times of India.* 2 vols., crown 8vo, cloth extra, with many Illustrations, and a Route Map.

This Work gives a full and detailed account of the author's adventurous ride of which an epitome appeared in the *Times.*

Atlantic Islands as Resorts of Health and Pleasure. By S. G. W. BENJAMIN, Author of "Contemporary Art in Europe," &c. Royal 8vo, cloth extra, with upwards of 150 Illustrations, 16*s.*

Atmosphere (The). *See* FLAMMARION.

Auld Lang Syne. By the Author of "Wreck of the Grosvenor." 2 vols., crown 8vo, 21*s.*

BAKER (Lieut.-Gen. Valentine, Pasha). *See* "War in Bulgaria."

Barton Experiment (The). By the Author of "Helen's Babies." 1s.

THE BAYARD SERIES,

Edited by the late J. HAIN FRISWELL.

Comprising Pleasure Books of Literature produced in the Choicest Style as Companionable Volumes at Home and Abroad.

"We can hardly imagine better books for boys to read or for men to ponder over."—*Times.*

Price 2s. 6d. each Volume, complete in itself, flexible cloth extra, gilt edges, with silk Headbands and Registers.

The Story of the Chevalier Bayard. By M. DE BERVILLE.

De Joinville's St. Louis, King of France.

The Essays of Abraham Cowley, including all his Prose Works.

Abdallah; or the Four Leaves. By EDOUARD LABOULLAYE.

Table-Talk and Opinions of Napoleon Buonaparte.

Vathek: An Oriental Romance. By WILLIAM BECKFORD.

The King and the Commons. A Selection of Cavalier and Puritan Songs. Edited by Prof. MORLEY.

Words of Wellington: Maxims and Opinions of the Great Duke.

Dr. Johnson's Rasselas, Prince of Abyssinia. With Notes.

Hazlitt's Round Table. With Biographical Introduction.

The Religio Medici, Hydriotaphia, and the Letter to a Friend. By Sir THOMAS BROWNE, Knt.

Ballad Poetry of the Affections. By ROBERT BUCHANAN.

Coleridge's Christabel, and other Imaginative Poems. With Preface by ALGERNON C. SWINBURNE.

Lord Chesterfield's Letters, Sentences, and Maxims. With Introduction by the Editor, and Essay on Chesterfield by M. DE STE.-BEUVE, of the French Academy.

Essays in Mosaic. By THOS. BALLANTYNE.

My Uncle Toby; his Story and his Friends. Edited by P. FITZGERALD.

Reflections; or, Moral Sentences and Maxims of the Duke de la Rochefoucauld.

*Socrates: Memoirs for English Readers from Xenophon's Memo*rabilia. By EDW. LEVIEN.

Prince Albert's Golden Precepts.

A Case containing 12 Volumes, price 31s. 6d.; or the Case separately, price 3s. 6d.

Beauty and the Beast. An Old Tale retold, with Pictures by B. V. B. Demy 4to, cloth extra, novel binding. 10 Illustrations in Colours (in same style as those in the First Edition of "Story without an End"). 12s. 6d.

Beumer's German Copybooks. In six gradations at 4*d.* each.

Biart (Lucien). See "Adventures of a Young Naturalist." "My Rambles in the New World," "The Two Friends."

Bickersteth's Hymnal Companion to Book of Common Prayer.

The Original Editions, containing 403 Hymns, always kept in Print.

Revised and Enlarged Edition, containing 550 Hymns—

*** *The Revised Editions are entirely distinct from, and cannot be used with, the original editions.*

		s.	*d*
7A	Medium 32mo, cloth limp	0	8
7B	ditto roan	1	2
7C	ditto morocco or calf	2	6
8A	Super-royal 32mo, cloth limp	1	0
8B	ditto red edges	1	2
8C	ditto roan	2	2
8D	ditto morocco or calf	3	6
9A	Crown 8vo, cloth, red edges	3	0
9B	ditto roan	4	0
9C	ditto morocco or calf	6	0
10A	Crown 8vo, with Introduction and Notes, red edges	4	0
10B	ditto roan	5	0
10C	ditto morocco	7	6
11A	Penny Edition in Wrapper	0	1
11B	ditto cloth	0	2
11C	With Prayer Book, cloth	0	9
11D	ditto roan	1	0
11E	ditto morocco	2	6
11F	ditto persian	1	6
12A	Crown 8vo, with Tunes, cloth, plain edges	4	0
12B	ditto ditto persian, red edges	6	6
12C	ditto ditto limp morocco, gilt edges	7	6
13A	Small 4to, for Organ	8	6
13B	ditto ditto limp russia	21	0
	Chant Book Supplement (Music)	1	6
	Ditto 4to, for Organ	3	6
14A	Tonic Sol-fa Edition	3	6
14B	ditto treble and alto only	1	0
5B	Chants only	1	6
5D	ditto 4to, for Organ	3	6
	The Church Mission Hymn-Book . . . . *per* 100	8	4
	Ditto ditto cloth . . . *each*	0	4

The "Hymnal Companion" may now be had in special bindings for presentation with and without the Common Prayer Book. A red line edition is ready. Lists on application.

Bickersteth (Rev. E. H., M.A.) The Reef and other Parables. 1 vol., square 8vo, with numerous very beautiful Engravings, 7*s.* 6*d.*

—— *The Clergyman in his Home.* Small post 8vo, 1*s.*

Bickersteth (Rev. E. H., M.A.) The Master's Home-Call; or, Brief Memorials of Alice Frances Bickersteth. 20th Thousand. 32mo, cloth gilt, 1*s.*

"They recall in a touching manner a character of which the religious beauty has a warmth and grace almost too tender to be definite."—*The Guardian.*

——— *The Shadow of the Rock.* A Selection of Religious Poetry. 18mo, cloth extra, 2*s.* 6*d.*

——— *The Shadowed Home and the Light Beyond.* 7th Edition, crown 8vo, cloth extra, 5*s.*

Bida. The Authorized Version of the Four Gospels, with the whole of the magnificent Etchings on Steel, after drawings by M. BIDA, in 4 vols., appropriately bound in cloth extra, price 3*l.* 3*s.* each.

Also the four volumes in two, bound in the best morocco, by Suttaby, extra gilt edges, 18*l.* 18*s.*, half-morocco, 12*l.* 12*s.*

"Bida's Illustrations of the Gospels of St. Matthew and St. John have already received here and elsewhere a full recognition of their great merits."—*Times.*

Bidwell (C. T.) The Balearic Islands. Illustrations and a Map. Crown 8vo, cloth, 10*s.* 6*d.*

——— *The Cost of Living Abroad.* Crown 8vo, 6*s.*

Black (Wm.) Three Feathers. Small post 8vo, cloth extra, 6*s.*

——— *Lady Silverdale's Sweetheart, and other Stories.* 1 vol., small post 8vo, 6*s.*

——— *Kilmeny: a Novel.* Small post 8vo, cloth, 6*s.*

——— *In Silk Attire.* 3rd Edition, small post 8vo, 6*s.*

——— *A Daughter of Heth.* 11th Edition, small post 8vo, 6*s.*

Blackmore (R. D.) Lorna Doone. 10th Edition, cr. 8vo, 6*s.*

"The reader at times holds his breath, so graphically yet so simply does John Ridd tell his tale."—*Saturday Review.*

——— *Alice Lorraine.* 1 vol., small post 8vo, 6th Edition, 6*s.*

——— *Clara Vaughan.* Revised Edition, 6*s.*

——— *Cradock Nowell.* New Edition, 6*s.*

——— *Cripps the Carrier.* 3rd Edition, small post 8vo, 6*s.*

Blossoms from the King's Garden: Sermons for Children. By the Rev. C. BOSANQUET. 2nd Edition, small post 8vo, cloth extra, 6s.

Blue Banner (The); or, The Adventures of a Mussulman, a Christian, and a Pagan, in the time of the Crusades and Mongol Conquest. By LEON CAHUN. Translated from the French by W. COLLETT SANDARS. With Seventy-six Wood Engravings. 1 vol., square imperial 16mo, cloth extra, 7*s.* 6*d.*

Book of English Elegies. Small post 8vo, cloth extra, 5*s.*

Book of the Play. By DUTTON COOK. 2 vols., crown 8vo, 24*s.*

Bradford (Wm.) The Arctic Regions. Illustrated with Photographs, taken on an Art Expedition to Greenland. With Descriptive Narrative by the Artist. In One Volume, royal broadside, 25 inches by 20, beautifully bound in morocco extra, price Twenty-Five Guineas.

Brave Men in Action. By S. J. MACKENNA. Crown 8vo, 480 pp., cloth, 10*s.* 6*d.*

Breck (Samuel). *See* "Recollections."

Browning (Mrs. E. B.) The Rhyme of the Duchess May. Demy 4to, Illustrated with Eight Photographs, after Drawings by CHARLOTTE M. B. MORRELL. 21*s.*

Bryant (W. C., assisted by S. H. Gay) A Popular History of the United States. About 4 vols., to be profusely Illustrated with Engravings on Steel and Wood, after Designs by the best Artists. Vol. I., super-royal 8vo, cloth extra, gilt, 42*s.*, is ready.

Burnaby (Capt.) *See* "On Horseback."

Burton (Captain R. F.) Two Trips to Gorilla Land and the Cataracts of the Congo. By Captain R. F. BURTON. 2 vols, demy 8vo, with numerous Illustrations and Map, cloth extra, 28*s.*

Butler (W. F.) The Great Lone Land; an Account of the Red River Expedition, 1869-70, and Subsequent Travels and Adventures in the Manitoba Country, and a Winter Journey across the Saskatchewan Valley to the Rocky Mountains. With Illustrations and Map. Fifth and Cheaper Edition, crown 8vo, cloth extra, 7*s.* 6*d.*

—— *The Wild North Land; the Story of a Winter* Journey with Dogs across Northern North America. Demy 8vo, cloth, with numerous Woodcuts and a Map, 4th Edition, 18*s.* Cr. 8vo, 7*s.* 6*d.*

—— *Akim-foo: the History of a Failure.* Demy 8vo, cloth, 2nd Edition, 16*s.* Also, in crown 8vo, 7*s.* 6*d.*

By Land and Ocean; or, The Journal and Letters of a Tour round the World by a Young Girl, who went *alone* to Victoria, New Zealand, Sydney, Singapore, China, Japan, and across the Continent of America home. By F. L. RAINS. Crown 8vo, cloth, 7*s.* 6*d.*

CABUL: the Ameer, his Country, and his People. By PHIL ROBINSON, Special Correspondent of the *Daily Telegraph*, with the Army of Afghanistan. With a Portrait of Shere Ali, and a Map of the Seat of the Anglo-Russian Question. 16mo, 1*s.* Fourth Thousand.

Cadogan (Lady A.) Illustrated Games of Patience. Twenty-four Diagrams in Colours, with Descriptive Text. Foolscap 4to, cloth extra, gilt edges, 3rd Edition, 12*s.* 6*d.*

Cahun (Leon) Adventures of Captain Mago. *See* "Adventures."

—— *Blue Banner*, which see.

Carbon Process (A Manual of). *See* LIESEGANG.

Ceramic Art. *See* JACQUEMART.

Changed Cross (The), and other Religious Poems. 16mo, 2*s.* 6*d.*

Child of the Cavern (The); or, Strange Doings Underground. By JULES VERNE. Translated by W. H. G. KINGSTON, Author of "Snow Shoes and Canoes," "Peter the Whaler," "The Three Midshipmen," &c., &c., &c. Numerous Illustrations. Square crown 8vo, cloth extra, gilt edges, 7*s.* 6*d.*

Child's Play, with 16 Coloured Drawings by E. V. B. Printed on thick paper, with tints, 7*s*. 6*d*.

—— *New*. By E. V. B. Similar to the above. *See* New.

Chips from many Blocks. By ELIHU BURRITT, Author of "Walks in the Black Country," "From London to Land's End," "Sparks from the Anvil," &c. Demy 8vo, cloth extra, 6*s*.

Choice Editions of Choice Books. 2*s*. 6*d*. each, Illustrated by C. W. COPE, R.A., T. CRESWICK, R.A., E. DUNCAN, BIRKET FOSTER, J. C. HORSLEY, A.R.A., G. HICKS, R. REDGRAVE, R.A., C. STONEHOUSE, F. TAYLER, G. THOMAS, H. J. TOWNSHEND, E. H. WEHNERT, HARRISON WEIR, &c.

Bloomfield's Farmer's Boy.
Campbell's Pleasures of Hope.
Coleridge's Ancient Mariner.
Goldsmith's Deserted Village.
Goldsmith's Vicar of Wakefield.
Gray's Elegy in a Churchyard.
Keat's Eve of St. Agnes.
Milton's L'Allegro.
Poetry of Nature. Harrison Weir.
Rogers' (Sam.) Pleasures of Memory.
Shakespeare's Songs and Sonnets.
Tennyson's May Queen.
Elizabethan Poets.
Wordsworth's Pastoral Poems.

"Such works are a glorious beatification for a poet."—*Athenæum*.

Christian Activity. By ELEANOR C. PRICE. Cloth extra, 6*s*.

Christmas Story-teller (The). By Old Hands and New Ones. Crown 8vo, cloth extra, gilt edges, Fifty-two Illustrations, 10*s*. 6*d*.

Cobbett (William). A Biography. By EDWARD SMITH. 2 vols., crown 8vo, 25*s*.

Cook (D.) Young Mr. Nightingale. A Novel. 3 vols., 31*s*. 6*d*.

—— *The Banns of Marriage*. 2 vols., crown 8vo, 21*s*.

—— *Book of the Play*. 2 vols., crown 8vo, 24*s*.

—— *Doubleday's Children*. 3 vols., crown 8vo, 31*s*. 6*d*.

Coope (Col. W. Jesser) A Prisoner of War in Russia. By Col. W. JESSER COOPE, Imperial Ottoman Gendarmerie. Crown 8vo, cloth extra, 10*s*. 6*d*.

Covert Side Sketches: Thoughts on Hunting, with Different Packs and in Different Countries. By J. NEVITT FITT (H.H. of the *Sporting Gazette*, late of the *Field*). Crown 8vo, cloth extra, 10*s*. 6*d*.

Craik (Mrs.) The Adventures of a Brownie. By the Author of "John Halifax, Gentleman." With numerous Illustrations by Miss PATERSON. Square cloth, extra gilt edges, 5*s*.

Cripps the Carrier. 3rd Edition, 6*s*. *See* BLACKMORE.

Cruise of H.M.S. "Challenger" (The). By W. J. J. SPRY, R.N. With Route Map and many Illustrations. 6th Edition, demy 8vo, cloth, 18*s*. Cheap Edition, crown 8vo, small type, some of the Illustrations, 7*s*. 6*d*.

"The book before us supplies the information in a manner that leaves little to be desired. 'The Cruise of H.M.S. *Challenger*' is an exceedingly well-written, entertaining, and instructive book."—*United Service Gazette*.

"Agreeably written, full of information, and copiously illustrated."—*Broad Arrow*.

Curious Adventures of a Field Cricket. By Dr. ERNEST CANDÈZE. Translated by N. D'ANVERS. With numerous fine Illustrations. Crown 8vo, cloth extra, gilt edges, 7*s.* 6*d.*

DANA (R. H.) Two Years before the Mast and Twenty-Four years After. Revised Edition with Notes, 12mo, 6*s.*

Dana (Jas. D.) Corals and Coral Islands. Numerous Illustrations, Charts, &c. New and Cheaper Edition, with numerous important Additions and Corrections. Crown 8vo, cloth extra, 8*s.* 6*d.*

Daughter (A) of Heth. By W. BLACK. Crown 8vo, 6*s.*

Day of My Life (A); or, Every Day Experiences at Eton. By an ETON BOY, Author of "About Some Fellows." 16mo, cloth extra, 2*s.* 6*d.* 6th Thousand.

Dick Sands, the Boy Captain. By JULES VERNE. With nearly 100 Illustrations, cloth extra, gilt edges, 10*s.* 6*d.*

Discoveries of Prince Henry the Navigator, and their Results; being the Narrative of the Discovery by Sea, within One Century, of more than Half the World. By RICHARD HENRY MAJOR, F.S.A. Demy 8vo, with several Woodcuts, 4 Maps, and a Portrait of Prince Henry in Colours. Cloth extra, 15*s.*

Dodge (Mrs. M.) Hans Brinker; or, the Silver Skates. An entirely New Edition, with 59 Full-page and other Woodcuts. Square crown 8vo, cloth extra, 7*s.* 6*d.*; Text only, paper, 1*s.*

——— *Theophilus and Others.* 1 vol., small post 8vo, cloth extra, gilt, 3*s.* 6*d.*

Dogs of Assize. A Legal Sketch-Book in Black and White. Containing 6 Drawings by WALTER J. ALLEN. Folio, in wrapper, 6*s.* 8*d.*

Doré's Spain. *See* "Spain."

Dougall's (J. D.) Shooting; its Appliances, Practice, and Purpose. With Illustrations, cloth extra, 10*s.* 6*d.* *See* "Shooting."

EARLY History of the Colony of Victoria (The), from its Discovery to its Establishment as a Self-Governing Province of the British Empire. By FRANCIS P. LABILLIERE, Fellow of the Royal Colonial Institute, &c. 2 vols., crown 8vo, 21*s.*

Echoes of the Heart. *See* MOODY.

Elinor Dryden. By Mrs. MACQUOID. Crown 8vo, 6*s.*

English Catalogue of Books (The). Published during 1863 to 1871 inclusive, comprising also important American Publications.

This Volume, occupying over 450 Pages, shows the Titles of 32,000 New Books and New Editions issued during Nine Years, with the Size, Price, and Publisher's Name, the Lists of Learned Societies, Printing Clubs, and other Literary Associations, and the Books issued by them; as also the Publisher's Series and Collections—altogether forming an indispensable adjunct to the Bookseller's

Establishment, as well as to every Learned and Literary Club and Association. 30*s.*, half-bound.

*** Of the previous Volume, 1835 to 1862, very few remain on sale; as also of the Index Volume, 1837 to 1857.

English Catalogue of Books (The) Supplements, 1863, 1864, 1865, 3*s.* 6*d.* each; 1866, 1867, to 1878, 5*s.* each.

Eight Cousins. See ALCOTT.

English Writers, Chapters for Self-Improvement in English Literature. By the Author of "The Gentle Life," 6*s.*

Eton. See "Day of my Life," "Out of School," "About Some Fellows."

Evans (C.) Over the Hills and Far Away. By C. EVANS. One Volume, crown 8vo, cloth extra, 10*s.* 6*d.*

—— *A Strange Friendship.* Crown 8vo, cloth, 5*s.*

FAITH Gartney's Girlhood. By the Author of "The Gayworthy's." Fcap. with Coloured Frontispiece, 3*s.* 6*d.*

Familiar Letters on some Mysteries of Nature. See PHIPSON.

Favourite English Pictures. Containing Sixteen Permanent Autotype Reproductions of important Paintings of Modern British Artists. With letterpress descriptions. Atlas 4to, cloth extra, 2*l.* 2*s.*

Fern Paradise (The): A Plea for the Culture of Ferns. By F. G. HEATH. New Edition, entirely Rewritten, Illustrated with eighteen full-page and numerous other Woodcuts, and four permanent Photographs, large post 8vo, handsomely bound in cloth, 12*s.* 6*d.*

Fern World (The). By F. G. HEATH. Illustrated by Twelve Coloured Plates, giving complete Figures (Sixty-four in all) of every Species of British Fern, specially printed from Nature; by several full-page Engravings; and a permanent Photograph. Large post 8vo., cloth, gilt edges, 400 pp., 4th Edition, 12*s.* 6*d.*

Few (A) Hints on Proving Wills. Enlarged Edition, 1*s.*

Five Weeks in Greece. By J. F. YOUNG. Crown 8vo, 10*s.* 6*d.*

Flammarion (C.) The Atmosphere. Translated from the French of CAMILLE FLAMMARION. Edited by JAMES GLAISHER, F.R.S., Superintendent of the Magnetical and Meteorological Department of the Royal Observatory at Greenwich. With 10 Chromo-Lithographs and 81 Woodcuts. Royal 8vo, cloth extra, 30*s.*

Flooding of the Sahara (The). An Account of the project for opening direct communication with 38,000,000 people. With a description of North-West Africa and Soudan. By DONALD MACKENZIE. 8vo, cloth extra, with Illustrations, 10*s.* 6*d.*

Footsteps of the Master. See STOWE (MRS. BEECHER).

Forrest (John) Explorations in Australia. Being Mr. JOHN FORREST'S Personal Account of his Journeys. 1 vol., demy 8vo, cloth, with several Illustrations and 3 Maps, 16*s.*

Franc (*Maude Jeane*). The following form one Series, small post 8vo, in uniform cloth bindings:—

—— *Emily's Choice.* 5*s.*

—— *Hall's Vineyard.* 4*s.*

—— *John's Wife: a Story of Life in South Australia.* 4*s.*

—— *Marian; or, the Light of Some One's Home.* 5*s.*

—— *Silken Cords and Iron Fetters.* 4*s.*

—— *Vermont Vale.* 5*s.*

—— *Minnie's Mission.* 4*s.*

—— *Little Mercy.* 5*s.*

French Heiress (*A*) *in her own Chateau.* Crown 8vo, 12*s.* 6*d.*

Funny Foreigners and Eccentric Englishmen. 16 coloured comic Illustrations for Children. Fcap. folio, coloured wrappper, 4*s.*

GAMES of Patience. *See* CADOGAN.

Garvagh (*Lord*) *The Pilgrim of Scandinavia,* By LORD GARVAGH, B.A., Christ Church, Oxford, and Member of the Alpine Club. 8vo, cloth extra, with Illustrations, 10*s.* 6*d.*

Geary (*Grattan*). *See* "Asiatic Turkey."

Gentle Life (Queen Edition). 2 vols. in 1, small 4to, 10*s.* 6*d.*

THE GENTLE LIFE SERIES.

Price 6*s.* each; or in calf extra, price 10*s.* 6*d.*

The Gentle Life. Essays in aid of the Formation of Character of Gentlemen and Gentlewomen. 21st Edition.

"Deserves to be printed in letters of gold, and circulated in every house."—*Chambers' Journal.*

About in the World. Essays by the Author of "The Gentle Life."

"It is not easy to open it at any page without finding some handy idea."—*Morning Post.*

Like unto Christ. A New Translation of Thomas à Kempis' "De Imitatione Christi." With a Vignette from an Original Drawing by Sir THOMAS LAWRENCE. 2nd Edition.

"Could not be presented in a more exquisite form, for a more sightly volume was never seen."—*Illustrated London News.*

Familiar Words. An Index Verborum, or Quotation Handbook. Affording an immediate Reference to Phrases and Sentences that have become embedded in the English language. 3rd and enlarged Edition.

"The most extensive dictionary of quotation we have met with."—*Notes and Queries.*

The Gentle Life Series, continued:—

Essays by Montaigne. Edited, Compared, Revised, and Annotated by the Author of "The Gentle Life." With Vignette Portrait. 2nd Edition.

"We should be glad if any words of ours could help to bespeak a large circulation for this handsome attractive book."—*Illustrated Times.*

The Countess of Pembroke's Arcadia. Written by Sir PHILIP SIDNEY. Edited with Notes by Author of "The Gentle Life." 7*s.* 6*d.*

"All the best things in the Arcadia are retained intact in Mr. Friswell's edition." —*Examiner.*

The Gentle Life. 2nd Series, 8th Edition.

"There is not a single thought in the volume that does not contribute in some measure to the formation of a true gentleman."—*Daily News.*

Varia: Readings from Rare Books. Reprinted, by permission, from the *Saturday Review, Spectator,* &c.

"The books discussed in this volume are no less valuable than they are rare, and the compiler is entitled to the gratitude of the public."—*Observer.*

The Silent Hour: Essays, Original and Selected. By the Author of "The Gentle Life." 3rd Edition.

"All who possess 'The Gentle Life' should own this volume."—*Standard.*

Half-Length Portraits. Short Studies of Notable Persons. By J. HAIN FRISWELL. Small post 8vo, cloth extra, 6*s.*

Essays on English Writers, for the Self-improvement of Students in English Literature.

"To all (both men and women) who have neglected to read and study their native literature we would certainly suggest the volume before us as a fitting introduction." —*Examiner.*

Other People's Windows. By J. HAIN FRISWELL. 3rd Edition.

"The chapters are so lively in themselves, so mingled with shrewd views of human nature, so full of illustrative anecdotes, that the reader cannot fail to be amused."—*Morning Post.*

A Man's Thoughts. By J. HAIN FRISWELL.

German Primer. Being an Introduction to First Steps in German. By M. T. PREU. 2*s.* 6*d.*

Getting On in the World; or, Hints on Success in Life. By W. MATHEWS, LL.D. Small post 8vo, cloth, 2*s.* 6*d.*; gilt edges, 3*s.* 6*d.*

Gouffé. The Royal Cookery Book. By JULES GOUFFÉ; translated and adapted for English use by ALPHONSE GOUFFÉ, Head Pastrycook to her Majesty the Queen. Illustrated with large plates printed in colours. 161 Woodcuts, 8vo, cloth extra, gilt edges, 2*l.* 2*s.*

——— Domestic Edition, half-bound, 10*s.* 6*d.*

"By far the ablest and most complete work on cookery that has ever been submitted to the gastronomical world."—*Pall Mall Gazette.*

——— *The Book of Preserves; or, Receipts for Preparing and* Preserving Meat, Fish salt and smoked, Terrines, Gelatines, Vegetables, Fruit, Confitures, Syrups, Liqueurs de Famille, Petits Fours, Bonbons, &c., &c. 1 vol., royal 8vo, containing upwards of 500 Receipts and 34 Illustrations, 10*s.* 6*d.*

Gouffé. Royal Book of Pastry and Confectionery. By JULES GOUFFÉ, Chef-de-Cuisine of the Paris Jockey Club. Royal 8vo, Illustrated with 10 Chromo-lithographs and 137 Woodcuts, from Drawings by E. MONJAT. Cloth extra, gilt edges, 35*s.*

Gouraud (Mdlle.) Four Gold Pieces. Numerous Illustrations. Small post 8vo, cloth, 2*s.* 6*d.* *See also* Rose Library.

Government of M. Thiers. By JULES SIMON. Translated from the French. 2 vols., demy 8vo, cloth extra.

Gower (Lord Ronald) Handbook to the Art Galleries, Public and Private, of Belgium and Holland. 18mo, cloth, 5*s.*

—— *The Castle Howard Portraits.* 2 vols., folio, cl. extra, 6*l.* 6*s.*

Greek Grammar. See WALLER.

Guizot's History of France. Translated by ROBERT BLACK. Super-royal 8vo, very numerous Full-page and other Illustrations. In 5 vols., cloth extra, gilt, each 24*s.*

"It supplies a want which has long been felt, and ought to be in the hands of all students of history."—*Times.*

"Three-fourths of M. Guizot's great work are now completed, and the 'History of France,' which was so nobly planned, has been hitherto no less admirably executed."—*From long Review of Vol. III. in the Times.*

"M. Guizot's main merit is this, that, in a style at once clear and vigorous, he sketches the essential and most characteristic features of the times and personages described, and seizes upon every salient point which can best illustrate and bring out to view what is most significant and instructive in the spirit of the age described."—*Evening Standard,* Sept. 23, 1874.

—— *History of England.* In 3 vols. of about 500 pp. each, containing 60 to 70 Full-page and other Illustrations, cloth extra, gilt, 24*s.* each. Vol. III. in the press.

"For luxury of typography, plainness of print, and beauty of illustration, these volumes, of which but one has as yet appeared in English, will hold their own against any production of an age so luxurious as our own in everything, typography not excepted."—*Times.*

Guillemin. See "World of Comets."

Guyon (Mde.) Life. By UPHAM. 6th Edition, crown 8vo, 6*s.*

Guyot (A.) Physical Geography. By ARNOLD GUYOT, Author of "Earth and Man." In 1 volume, large 4to, 128 pp., numerous coloured Diagrams, Maps, and Woodcuts, price 10*s.* 6*d.*

HABITATIONS of Man in all Ages. See LE-DUC.

Hamilton (A. H. A., J.P.) See "Quarter Sessions."

Handbook to the Charities of London. See Low's.

—————— *Principal Schools of England. See* Practical.

Half-Hours of Blind Man's Holiday; or, Summer and Winter Sketches in Black & White. By W. W. FENN. 2 vols., cr. 8vo, 24*s.*

Half-Length Portraits. Short Studies of Notable Persons. By J. HAIN FRISWELL. Small post 8vo, cloth extra, 6*s.*

Hall (W. W.) How to Live Long; or, 1408 *Health Maxims,* Physical, Mental, and Moral. By W. W. HALL, A.M., M.D. Small post 8vo, cloth, 2*s.* Second Edition.

Hans Brinker; or, the Silver Skates. *See* DODGE.

Healy (M.) A Summer's Romance. Crown 8vo, cloth, 10*s.* 6*d.*

——— *The Home Theatre.* Small post 8vo, 3*s.* 6*d.*

Heart of Africa. Three Years' Travels and Adventures in the Unexplored Regions of Central Africa, from 1868 to 1871. By Dr. GEORG SCHWEINFURTH. Translated by ELLEN E. FREWER. With an Introduction by WINWOOD READE. An entirely New Edition, revised and condensed by the Author. Numerous Illustrations, and large Map. 2 vols., crown 8vo, cloth, 15*s.*

Heath (F. G.). *See* "Fern World," "Fern Paradise," "Our Woodland Trees."

Heber's (Bishop) Illustrated Edition of Hymns. With upwards of 100 beautiful Engravings. Small 4to, handsomely bound, 7*s.* 6*d.* Morocco, 18*s.* 6*d.* and 21*s.* An entirely New Edition.

Hector Servadac. *See* VERNE. The heroes of this story were carried away through space on the Comet "Gallia," and their adventures are recorded with all Jules Verne's characteristic spirit. With nearly 100 Illustrations, cloth extra, gilt edges, 10*s.* 6*d.*

Henderson (A.) Latin Proverbs and Quotations; with Translations and Parallel Passages, and a copious English Index. By ALFRED HENDERSON. Fcap. 4to, 530 pp., 10*s.* 6*d.*

History and Handbook of Photography. Translated from the French of GASTON TISSANDIER. Edited by J. THOMSON. Imperial 16mo, over 300 pages, 70 Woodcuts, and Specimens of Prints by the best Permanent Processes, cloth extra, 6*s.* Second Edition, with an Appendix by the late Mr. HENRY FOX TALBOT, giving an account of his researches.

History of a Crime (The); Deposition of an Eye-witness. By VICTOR HUGO. 4 vols., crown 8vo, 42*s.*

——— *England.* *See* GUIZOT.

——— *France.* *See* GUIZOT.

——— *Russia.* *See* RAMBAUD.

——— *Merchant Shipping.* *See* LINDSAY.

——— *United States.* *See* BRYANT.

——— *Ireland.* By STANDISH O'GRADY. Vol. I. ready, 7*s.* 6*d.*

History and Principles of Weaving by Hand and by Power. With several hundred Illustrations. Reprinted with considerable additions from "Engineering," with a chapter on Lace-making Machinery. By ALFRED BARLOW. Royal 8vo, cloth extra, 1*l.* 5*s.*

Hitherto. By the Author of "The Gayworthys." New Edition, cloth extra, 3*s.* 6*d.* Also, in Rose Library, 2 vols., 2*s.*

Hofmann (Carl). A Practical Treatise on the Manufacture of Paper in all its Branches. Illustrated by 110 Wood Engravings, and 5 large Folding Plates. In 1 vol., 4to, cloth; about 400 pp., 3*l.* 13*s.* 6*d.*

How to Build a House. *See* LE-DUC.

How to Live Long. *See* HALL.

Hugo (Victor) "*Ninety-Three.*" Illustrated. Crown 8vo, 6*s.*

—— *Toilers of the Sea.* Crown 8vo. Illustrated, 6*s.*; fancy boards, 2*s.*; cloth, 2*s.* 6*d.*; On large paper with all the original Illustrations, 10*s.* 6*d.*

—— *See* "History of a Crime."

Hunting, Shooting, and Fishing; A Sporting Miscellany. Illustrated. Crown 8vo, cloth extra, 7*s.* 6*d.*

Hymnal Companion to Book of Common Prayer. *See* BICKERSTETH.

ILLUSTRATIONS of China and its People. By J. THOMSON, F.R.G.S. Being 200 permanent Photographs from the Author's Negatives, with Letterpress Descriptions of the Places and People represented. Four Volumes imperial 4to, each 3*l.* 3*s.*

In my Indian Garden. By PHIL. ROBINSON. With a Preface by EDWIN ARNOLD, M.A., C.S.I., &c. Crown 8vo, limp cloth, 3*s.* 6*d.*

Irish Bar. Comprising Anecdotes, Bon-Mots, and Biographical Sketches of the Bench and Bar of Ireland. By J. RODERICK O'FLANAGAN, Barrister-at-Law. 1 vol., crown 8vo, cloth.

JACQUEMART (A.) History of the Ceramic Art: Descriptive and Analytical Study of the Potteries of all Times and of all Nations. By ALBERT JACQUEMART. 200 Woodcuts by H. Catenacci and J. Jacquemart. 12 Steel-plate Engravings, and 1000 Marks and Monograms. Translated by Mrs. BURY PALLISER. In 1 vol., super-royal 8vo, of about 700 pp., cloth extra, gilt edges, 28*s.*

"This is one of those few gift-books which, while they can certainly lie on a table and look beautiful, can also be read through with real pleasure and profit."—*Times.*

KENNEDY'S (Capt. W. R.) Sporting Adventures in the Pacific. With Illustrations, demy 8vo, 18*s.*

—— *(Capt. A. W. M. Clark).* *See* "To the Arctic Regions."

Khedive's Egypt (The); or, The old House of Bondage under New Masters. By EDWIN DE LEON, Ex-Agent and Consul-General in Egypt. In 1 vol., demy 8vo, cloth extra, Third Edition, 18*s.*

Kingston (W. H. G.). *See* "Snow-Shoes."

—— *Child of the Cavern.*

—— *Two Supercargoes.*

—— *With Axe and Rifle.*

Koldewey (Capt.) The Second North German Polar Expedition in the Year 1869-70, of the Ships "Germania" and "Honsa," under command of Captain Koldewey. Edited and condensed by H. W. BATES, Esq. Numerous Woodcuts, Maps, and Chromo-lithographs. Royal 8vo, cloth extra, 1*l.* 15*s.*

LADY Silverdale's Sweetheart. 6*s*. *See* BLACK.

Land of Bolivar (The); or, War, Peace, and Adventure in the Republic of Venezuela. By JAMES MUDIE SPENCE, F.R.G.S., F.Z.S. 2 vols., demy 8vo, cloth extra, with numerous Woodcuts and Maps, 31*s*. 6*d*. Second Edition.

Landseer Gallery (The). Containing thirty-six Autotype Reproductions of Engravings from the most important early works of Sir EDWIN LANDSEER. With a Memoir of the Artist's Life, and Descriptions of the Plates. Imperial 4to, handsomely bound in cloth, gilt edges, 2*l*. 2*s*.

Le-Duc (V.) How to build a House. By VIOLLET-LE-DUC, Author of "The Dictionary of Architecture," &c. Numerous Illustrations, Plans, &c. Medium 8vo, cloth, gilt, 12*s*.

——— *Annals of a Fortress.* Numerous Illustrations and Diagrams. Demy 8vo, cloth extra, 15*s*.

——— *The Habitations of Man in all Ages.* By E. VIOLLET-LE-DUC. Illustrated by 103 Woodcuts. Translated by BENJAMIN BUCKNALL, Architect. 8vo, cloth extra, 16*s*.

——— *Lectures on Architecture.* By VIOLLET-LE-DUC. Translated from the French by BENJAMIN BUCKNALL, Architect. In 2 vols., royal 8vo, 3*l*. 3*s*. Also in Parts, 10*s*. 6*d*. each.

——— *Mont Blanc: a Treatise on its Geodesical and Geological* Constitution—its Transformations, and the Old and Modern state of its Glaciers. By EUGENE VIOLLET-LE-DUC. With 120 Illustrations. Translated by B. BUCKNALL. 1 vol., demy 8vo, 14*s*.

——— *On Restoration;* with a Notice of his Works by CHARLES WETHERED. Crown 8vo, with a Portrait on Steel of VIOLLET-LE-DUC, cloth extra, 2*s*. 6*d*.

Lenten Meditations. In Two Series, each complete in itself. By the Rev. CLAUDE BOSANQUET, Author of "Blossoms from the King's Garden." 16mo, cloth, First Series, 1*s*. 6*d*.; Second Series, 2*s*.

Liesegang (Dr. Paul E.) A Manual of the Carbon Process of Photography, and its use in Making Enlargements, &c. Translated from the Sixth German Edition by R. B. MARSTON. Demy 8vo, half-bound, with Illustrations, 4*s*.

Life and Letters of the Honourable Charles Sumner (The). 2 vols., royal 8vo, cloth. The Letters give full description of London Society—Lawyers—Judges—Visits to Lords Fitzwilliam, Leicester, Wharncliffe, Brougham—Association with Sydney Smith, Hallam, Macaulay, Dean Milman, Rogers, and Talfourd; also, a full Journal which Sumner kept in Paris. Second Edition, 36*s*.

Lindsay (W. S.) History of Merchant Shipping and Ancient Commerce. Over 150 Illustrations, Maps and Charts. In 4 vols., demy 8vo, cloth extra. Vols. 1 and 2, 21*s*.; vols. 3 and 4, 24*s*. each.

Lion Jack: a Story of Perilous Adventures amongst Wild Men and Beasts. Showing how Menageries are made. By P. T. BARNUM. With Illustrations. Crown 8vo, cloth extra, price 6*s.*

Little King; or, the Taming of a Young Russian Count. By S. BLANDY. Translated from the French. 64 Illustrations. Crown 8vo, cloth extra, gilt, 7*s.* 6*d.*

Little Mercy; or, For Better for Worse. By MAUDE JEANNE FRANC, Author of "Marian," "Vermont Vale," &c., &c. Small post 8vo, cloth extra, 4*s.*

Locker (A.) The Village Surgeon. A Fragment of Autobiography. By ARTHUR LOCKER. Crown 8vo, cloth, 3*s.* 6*d.*

Long (Col. C. Chaillé) Central Africa. Naked Truths of Naked People: an Account of Expeditions to Lake Victoria Nyanza and the Mabraka Niam-Niam. Demy 8vo, numerous Illustrations, 18*s.*

Lord Collingwood: a Biographical Study. By. W. DAVIS. With Steel Engraving of Lord Collingwood. Crown 8vo, 2*s.*

Lost Sir Massingberd. New Edition, 16mo, boards, coloured wrapper, 2*s.*

Low's German Series—

1. **The Illustrated German Primer.** Being the easiest introduction to the study of German for all beginners. 1*s.*
2. **The Children's own German Book.** A Selection of Amusing and Instructive Stories in Prose. Edited by Dr. A. L. MEISSNER, Professor of Modern Languages in the Queen's University in Ireland. Small post 8vo, cloth, 1*s.* 6*d.*
3. **The First German Reader, for Children from Ten to Fourteen.** Edited by Dr. A. L. MEISSNER. Small post 8vo, cloth, 1*s.* 6*d.*
4. **The Second German Reader.** Edited by Dr. A. L. MEISSNER, Small post 8vo, cloth, 1*s.* 6*d.*

Buchheim's Deutsche Prosa. Two Volumes, sold separately:—

5. **Schiller's Prosa.** Containing Selections from the Prose Works of Schiller, with Notes for English Students. By Dr. BUCHHEIM, Professor of the German Language and Literature, King's College, London. Small post 8vo, 2*s.* 6*d.*
6. **Goethe's Prosa.** Containing Selections from the Prose Works of Goethe, with Notes for English Students. By Dr. BUCHHEIM. Small post 8vo, 3*s.* 6*d.*

Low's Standard Library of Travel and Adventure. Crown 8vo, bound uniformly in cloth extra, price 7*s.* 6*d.*

1. **The Great Lone Land.** By W. F. BUTLER, C.B.
2. **The Wild North Land.** By W. F. BUTLER, C.B.
3. **How I found Livingstone.** By H. M. STANLEY.
4. **The Threshold of the Unknown Region.** By C. R. MARKHAM. (4th Edition, with Additional Chapters, 10*s.* 6*d.*)
5. **A Whaling Cruise to Baffin's Bay and the Gulf of Boothia.** By A. H. MARKHAM.

Low's Standard Library of Travel and Adventure, continued:—

6. **Campaigning on the Oxus.** By J. A. MacGahan.
7. **Akim-foo: the History of a Failure.** By Major W. F. Butler, C.B.
8. **Ocean to Ocean.** By the Rev. George M. Grant. With Illustrations.
9. **Cruise of the Challenger.** By W. J. J. Spry, R.N.
10. **Schweinfurth's Heart of Africa.** 2 vols., 15*s.*

Low's Standard Novels. Crown 8vo, 6*s.* each, cloth extra.

Three Feathers. By William Black.
A Daughter of Heth. 13th Edition. By W. Black. With Frontispiece by F. Walker, A.R.A.
Kilmeny. A Novel. By W. Black.
In Silk Attire. By W. Black.
Lady Silverdale's Sweetheart. By W. Black.
Alice Lorraine. By R. D. Blackmore.
Lorna Doone. By R. D. Blackmore. 8th Edition.
Cradock Nowell. By R. D. Blackmore.
Clara Vaughan. By R. D. Blackmore.
Cripps the Carrier. By R. D. Blackmore.
Innocent. By Mrs. Oliphant. Eight Illustrations.
Work. A Story of Experience. By Louisa M. Alcott. Illustrations. *See also* Rose Library.
Mistress Judith. A Cambridgeshire Story. By C. C. Fraser-Tytler.
Never Again. By Dr. Mayo, Author of "Kaloolah."
Ninety-Three. By Victor Hugo. Numerous Illustrations.
My Wife and I. By Mrs. Beecher Stowe.
Wreck of the Grosvenor. By W. Clark Russell.
Elinor Dryden. By Mrs. Macquoid.

Low's Handbook to the Charities of London for 1877. Edited and revised to July, 1877, by C. Mackeson, F.S.S., Editor of "A Guide to the Churches of London and its Suburbs," &c. 1*s.*

MACGAHAN (J. A.) Campaigning on the Oxus, and the Fall of Khiva. With Map and numerous Illustrations, 4th Edition, small post 8vo, cloth extra, 7*s.* 6*d.*

—— *Under the Northern Lights; or, the Cruise of the* "Pandora" to Peel's Straits, in Search of Sir John Franklin's Papers. With Illustrations by Mr. De Wylde, who accompanied the Expedition. Demy 8vo, cloth extra, 18*s.*

Macgregor (John) "Rob Roy" on the Baltic. 3rd Edition, small post 8vo, 2*s.* 6*d.*

—— *A Thousand Miles in the "Rob Roy" Canoe.* 11th Edition, small post 8vo, 2*s.* 6*d.*

—— *Description of the "Rob Roy" Canoe,* with Plans, &c., 1*s.*

—— *The Voyage Alone in the Yawl "Rob Roy."* New Edition, thoroughly revised, with additions, small post 8vo, 5*s.*

Mackenzie (D). The Flooding of the Sahara. An Account of the Project for opening direct communication with 38,000,000 people. With a Description of North-West Africa and Soudan. By DONALD MACKENZIE. 8vo, cloth extra, with Illustrations, 10*s.* 6*d.*

Macquoid (Mrs.) Elinor Dryden. Crown 8vo, cloth, 6*s.*

Markham (A. H.) The Cruise of the "Rosario." By A. H. MARKHAM, R.N. 8vo, cloth extra, with Map and Illustrations.

——— *A Whaling Cruise to Baffin's Bay and the Gulf of* Boothia. With an Account of the Rescue by his Ship, of the Survivors of the Crew of the "Polaris;" and a Description of Modern Whale Fishing. 3rd and Cheaper Edition, crown 8vo, 2 Maps and several Illustrations, cloth extra, 7*s.* 6*d.*

Markham (C. R.) The Threshold of the Unknown Region. Crown 8vo, with Four Maps, 4th Edition, with Additional Chapters, giving the History of our present Expedition, as far as known, and an Account of the Cruise of the "Pandora." Cloth extra, 10*s.* 6*d.*

Maury (Commander) Physical Geography of the Sea, and its Meteorology. Being a Reconstruction and Enlargement of his former Work, with Charts and Diagrams. New Edition, crown 8vo, 6*s.*

Men of Mark: a Gallery of Contemporary Portraits of the most Eminent Men of the Day taken from Life, especially for this publication, price 1*s.* 6*d.* monthly. Vols. I., II., and III. handsomely bound, cloth, gilt edges, 25*s.* each.

Mercy Philbrick's Choice. Small post 8vo, 3*s.* 6*d.*

"The story is of a high character, and the play of feeling is very subtilely and cleverly wrought out."—*British Quarterly Review.*

Michael Strogoff. 10*s.* 6*d.* *See* VERNE.

Mistress Judith. A Cambridgeshire Story. By C. C. FRASER-TYTLER, Author of "Jasmine Leigh." A New and Cheaper Edition in 1 vol., small post 8vo, cloth extra, 6*s.*

Mitford (Miss). See "Our Village."

Mohr (E.) To the Victoria Falls of the Zambesi. By EDWARD MOHR. Translated by N. D'ANVÉRS. Numerous Full-page and other Woodcut Illustrations, four Chromo-lithographs, and Map. Demy 8vo, cloth extra, 24*s.*

Mongolia, Travels in. See PREJEVALSKY.

Montaigne's Essays. See Gentle Life Series.

Mont Blanc. See LE-DUC.

Moody (Emma) Echoes of the Heart. A Collection of upwards of 200 Sacred Poems. 16mo, cloth, gilt edges, price 3*s.* 6*d.*

My Brother Jack; or, The Story of Whatd'yecallem. Written by Himself. From the French of ALPHONSE DAUDET. Illustrated by P. PHILIPPOTEAUX. Square imperial 16mo, cloth extra, 7*s.* 6*d.*

"He would answer to Hi! or to any loud cry,
To What-you-may-call-'em, or What was his name;
But especially Thingamy-jig."—*Hunting of the Snark.*

My Rambles in the New World. By LUCIEN BIART, Author of "The Adventures of a Young Naturalist." Translated by MARY DE HAUTEVILLE. Crown 8vo, cloth extra. Numerous Full-page Illustrations, 7*s*. 6*d*.

NARES (Sir G. S., K.C.B.) Narrative of a Voyage to the Polar Sea during 1875-76, in H.M.'s Ships "Alert" and "Discovery." By Captain Sir G. S. NARES, R.N., K.C.B., F.R.S. Published by permission of the Lords Commissioners of the Admiralty. With Notes on the Natural History, edited by H. W. FEILDEN, F.G.S., C.M.Z.S., F.R.G.S., Naturalist to the Expedition. Two Volumes, demy 8vo, with numerous Woodcut Illustrations and Photographs, &c. 4th Edition, 2*l*. 2*s*.

New Child's Play (A). Sixteen Drawings by E. V. B. Beautifully printed in colours, 4to, cloth extra, 12*s*. 6*d*.

New Ireland. By A. M. SULLIVAN, M.P. for Louth. 2 vols., demy 8vo, cloth extra, 30*s*. One of the main objects which the Author has had in view in writing this work has been to lay before England and the world a faithful history of Ireland, in a series of descriptive sketches of the episodes in Ireland's career during the last quarter of a century. Cheaper Edition, 1 vol., crown 8vo, 8*s*. 6*d*.

New Novels.

An Old Story of My Farming Days. By FRITZ REUTER, Author of "In the Year '13." 3 vols., 1*l*. 11*s*. 6*d*.

Cressida. By M. B. THOMAS. 3 vols., 1*l*. 11*s*. 6*d*.

Elizabeth Eden. 3 vols., 1*l*. 11*s*. 6*d*.

The Martyr of Glencree. A Story of the Persecutions in Scotland in the Reign of Charles the Second. By R. SOMERS. 3 vols., 1*l*. 11*s*. 6*d*.

The Cossacks. By COUNT TOLSTOY. Translated from the Russian by EUGENE SCHUYLER, Author of "Turkistan." 2 vols., 1*l*. 1*s*.

A Hero of the Pen. 2 vols. By WERNER. Translated by Mrs. S. PHILLIPS. 21*s*.

The Braes of Yarrow. By C. GIBBON. 3 vols., 1*l*. 11*s*. 6*d*.

Auld Lang Syne. By the Author of "The Wreck of the Grosvenor." 2 vols., 1*l*. 1*s*.

A Life's Hazard; or, The Outlaw of Wentworth Waste. By H. ESMOND. 3 vols., 1*l*. 11*s*. 6*d*.

Rare Pale Margaret. 2 vols., 1*l*. 1*s*.

A French Heiress. By the Author of "One Only," &c. With Illustrations, 12*s*. 6*d*.

New Testament. The Authorized English Version; with various readings from the most celebrated Manuscripts. Cloth flexible, gilt edges, 2*s*. 6*d*.; cheaper style, 2*s*.; or sewed, 1*s*. 6*d*.

Noble Words and Noble Deeds. Translated from the French of E. MULLER, by DORA LEIGH. Containing many Full-page Illustrations by PHILIPPOTEAUX. Square imperial 16mo, cloth extra, 7*s.* 6*d.*

"This is a book which will delight the young. . . . We cannot imagine a nicer present than this book for children."—*Standard.*

"Is certain to become a favourite with young people."—*Court Journal.*

Notes and Sketches of an Architect taken during a Journey in the North-West of Europe. Translated from the French of FELIX NARJOUX. 214 Full-page and other Illustrations. Demy 8vo, cloth extra, 16*s.*

"His book is vivacious and sometimes brilliant. It is admirably printed and illustrated."—*British Quarterly Review.*

Notes on Fish and Fishing. By the Rev. J. J. MANLEY, M.A. With Illustrations, crown 8vo, cloth extra, leatherette binding, 10*s.* 6*d.*

"We commend the work."—*Field.*

"He has a page for every day in the year, or nearly so, and there is not a dull one amongst them."—*Notes and Queries.*

"A pleasant and attractive volume."—*Graphic.*

"Brightly and pleasantly written."—*John Bull.*

Nursery Playmates (Prince of.) 217 Coloured pictures for Children by eminent Artists. Folio, in coloured boards, 6*s.*

OCEAN to Ocean: Sandford Fleming's Expedition through Canada in 1872. By the Rev. GEORGE M. GRANT. With Illustrations. Revised and enlarged Edition, crown 8vo, cloth, 7*s.* 6*d.*

Old-Fashioned Girl. See ALCOTT.

Oleographs. (Catalogues and price lists on application.)

Oliphant (Mrs.) Innocent. A Tale of Modern Life. By Mrs. OLIPHANT, Author of "The Chronicles of Carlingford," &c., &c. With Eight Full-page Illustrations, small post 8vo, cloth extra, 6*s.*

On Horseback through Asia Minor. By Capt. FRED BURNABY, Royal Horse Guards, Author of "A Ride to Khiva." 2 vols., 8vo, with three Maps and Portrait of Author, 6th Edition, 38*s.* This work describes a ride of over 2000 miles through the heart of Asia Minor, and gives an account of five months with Turks, Circassians, Christians, and Devil-worshippers. Cheaper Edition, crown 8vo, 10*s.* 6*d.*

On Restoration. See LE-DUC.

On Trek in the Transvaal; or, Over Berg and Veldt in South Africa. By H. A. ROCHE. Crown 8vo, cloth, 10*s.* 6*d.* 4th Edition.

Our Little Ones in Heaven. Edited by the Rev. H. ROBBINS. With Frontispiece after Sir JOSHUA REYNOLDS. Fcap., cloth extra, New Edition—the 3rd, with Illustrations, 5*s.*

Our Village. By MARY RUSSELL MITFORD. Illustrated with Frontispiece Steel Engraving, and 12 full-page and 157 smaller Cuts of Figure Subjects and Scenes, from Drawings by W. H. J. BOOT and C. O. MURRAY. Chiefly from Sketches made by these Artists in the neighbourhood of "Our Village." Crown 4to, cloth extra, gilt edges, 21*s.*

Our Woodland Trees. By F. G. HEATH. Large post 8vo, cloth, gilt edges, uniform with "Fern World" and "Fern Paradise," by the same Author. 8 Coloured Plates and 20 Woodcuts, 12*s.* 6*d.*

Out of School at Eton. Being a collection of Poetry and Prose Writings. By SOME PRESENT ETONIANS. Foolscap 8vo, cloth, 3*s.* 6*d.*

PAINTERS of All Schools. By LOUIS VIARDOT, and other Writers. 500 pp., super-royal 8vo, 20 Full-page and 70 smaller Engravings, cloth extra, 25*s.* A New Edition is being issued in Half-crown parts, with fifty additional portraits, cloth, gilt edges, 31*s.* 6*d.*

"A handsome volume, full of information and sound criticism."—*Times.*

"Almost an encyclopædia of painting. . . . . It may be recommended as a handy and elegant guide to beginners in the study of the history of art."—*Saturday Review.*

Palliser (Mrs.) A History of Lace, from the Earliest Period. A New and Revised Edition, with additional cuts and text, upwards of 100 Illustrations and coloured Designs. 1 vol. 8vo, 1*l.* 1*s.*

"One of the most readable books of the season; permanently valuable, always interesting, often amusing, and not inferior in all the essentials of a gift book."—*Times.*

—— *Historic Devices, Badges, and War Cries.* 8vo, 1*l.* 1*s.*

—— *The China Collector's Pocket Companion.* With upwards of 1000 Illustrations of Marks and Monograms. 2nd Edition, with Additions. Small post 8vo, limp cloth, 5*s.*

"We scarcely need add that a more trustworthy and convenient handbook does not exist, and that others besides ourselves will feel grateful to Mrs. Palliser for the care and skill she has bestowed upon it."—*Academy.*

Petites Leçons de Conversation et de Grammaire: Oral and Conversational Method; being Little Lessons introducing the most Useful Topics of Daily Conversation, upon an entirely new principle, &c. By F. JULIEN, French Master at King Edward the Sixth's Grammar School, Birmingham. Author of "The Student's French Examiner," which see.

Phelps (Miss) Gates Ajar. 32mo, 6*d.*

—— *Men, Women, and Ghosts.* 12mo, sewed, 1*s.* 6*d.*; cl., 2*s.*

—— *Hedged In.* 12mo, sewed, 1*s.* 6*d.*; cloth, 2*s.*

—— *Silent Partner.* 5*s.*

—— *Trotty's Wedding Tour.* Small post 8vo, 3*s.* 6*d.*

—— *What to Wear.* Fcap. 8vo, fancy boards, 1*s.*

Phillips (L.) Dictionary of Biographical Reference. 8vo, 1*l.* 11*s.* 6*d.*

Phipson (Dr. T. L.) Familiar Letters on some Mysteries of Nature and Discoveries in Science. Crown 8vo, cloth extra, 7*s.* 6*d.*

Photography (History and Handbook of). *See* TISSANDIER.

Picture Gallery of British Art (The). 38 Permanent Photographs after the most celebrated English Painters. With Descriptive Letterpress. Vols. 1 to 5, cloth extra, 18*s.* each. Vol. 6 for 1877, commencing New Series, demy folio, 31*s.* 6*d.* Monthly Parts, 1*s.* 6*d.*

Pike (N.) Sub-Tropical Rambles in the Land of the Aphanapteryx. In 1 vol., demy 8vo, 18*s.* Profusely Illustrated from the Author's own Sketches. Also with Maps and Meteorological Charts.

Placita Anglo-Normannica. The Procedure and Constitution of the Anglo-Norman Courts (WILLIAM I.—RICHARD I.), as shown by Contemporaneous Records; all the Reports of the Litigation of the period, as recorded in the Chronicles and Histories of the time, being gleaned and literally transcribed. With Explanatory Notes, &c. By M. M. BIGELOW. Demy 8vo, cloth, 14*s.*

Plutarch's Lives. An Entirely New and Library Edition. Edited by A. H. CLOUGH, Esq. 5 vols., 8vo, 2*l.* 10*s.*; half-morocco, gilt top, 3*l.* Also in 1 vol., royal 8vo, 800 pp., cloth extra, 18*s.*; half-bound, 21*s.*

—— *Morals.* Uniform with Clough's Edition of "Lives of Plutarch." Edited by Professor GOODWIN. 5 vols., 8vo, 3*l.* 3*s.*

Poe (E. A.) The Works of. 4 vols., 2*l.* 2*s.*

Poems of the Inner Life. A New Edition, Revised, with many additional Poems, inserted by permission of the Authors. Small post 8vo, cloth, 5*s.*

Poganuc People: their Loves and Lives. By Mrs. BEECHER STOWE. Crown 8vo, cloth, 10*s.* 6*d.*

Polar Expeditions. See KOLDEWEY, MARKHAM, MACGAHAN, and NARES.

Pottery: how it is Made, its Shape and Decoration. Practical Instructions for Painting on Porcelain and all kinds of Pottery with vitrifiable and common Oil Colours. With a full Bibliography of Standard Works upon the Ceramic Art. By G. WARD NICHOLS. 42 Illustrations, crown 8vo, red edges, 6*s.*

Practical (A) Handbook to the Principal Schools of England. By C. E. PASCOE. Showing the cost of living at the Great Schools, Scholarships, &c., &c. New Edition corrected to 1878, crown 8vo, cloth extra, 3*s.* 6*d.*

"This is an exceedingly useful work, and one that was much wanted."—*Examiner.*

Prejevalsky (N. M.) Travels in Mongolia. By N. M. PREJEVALSKY, Lieutenant-Colonel, Russian Staff. Translated by E. DELMAR MORGAN, F.R.G.S., and Annotated by Colonel YULE, C.B. 2 vols., demy 8vo, cloth extra, numerous Illustrations and Maps, 2*l.* 2*s.*

—— *From Kulja, across the Tian Shan to Lob-Nor.* Translated by E. DELMAR MORGAN, F.R.G.S. With Notes and Introduction by SIR DOUGLAS FORSYTH, K.C.S.I. 1 vol., demy 8vo, with a Map.

Price (Sir Rose, Bart.). See "Two Americas."

Prince Ritto; or, The Four-leaved Shamrock. By FANNY W. CURREY. With 10 Full-page Fac-simile Reproductions of Original Drawings by HELEN O'HARA. Demy 4to, cloth extra, gilt, 10*s.* 6*d.*

Prisoner of War in Russia. *See* COOPE.

Publishers' Circular (The), and General Record of British and Foreign Literature. Published on the 1st and 15th of every Month.

QUARTER Sessions, from Queen Elizabeth to Queen Anne: Illustrations of Local Government and History. Drawn from Original Records (chiefly of the County of Devon). By A. H. A. HAMILTON. Crown 8vo, cloth, 10*s.* 6*d.*

RALSTON (W. R. S.) Early Russian History. Four Lectures delivered at Oxford by W. R. S. RALSTON, M.A. Crown 8vo, cloth extra, 5*s.*

Rambaud (Alfred). History of Russia, from its Origin to the Year 1877. With Six Maps. Translated by Mrs. L. B. LANG. 2 vols. demy 8vo, cloth extra.

Recollections of Samuel Breck, the American Pepys. With Passages from his Note-Books (1771—1862). Crown 8vo, cloth, 10*s.* 6*d.*

"The book is admirable."—*Standard.*

Recollections of Writers. By CHARLES and MARY COWDEN CLARKE. Authors of "The Concordance to Shakespeare," &c.; with Letters of CHARLES LAMB, LEIGH HUNT, DOUGLAS JERROLD, and CHARLES DICKENS; and a Preface by MARY COWDEN CLARKE. Crown 8vo, cloth, 10*s.* 6*d.*

Reynard the Fox. The Prose Translation by the late THOMAS ROSCOE. With about 100 exquisite Illustrations on Wood, after designs by A. J. ELWES. Imperial 16mo, cloth extra, 7*s.* 6*d.*

Robinson (Phil.). *See* "In my Indian Garden."

Roche (Mrs. H.). *See* "On Trek in the Transvaal."

Rochefoucauld's Reflections. Bayard Series, 2*s.* 6*d.*

Rogers (S.) Pleasures of Memory. *See* "Choice Editions of Choice Books." 2*s.* 6*d.*

Rohlfs (Dr. G.) Adventures in Morocco, and Journeys through the Oases of Draa and Tafilet. By Dr. G. ROHLFS. Demy 8vo, Map, and Portrait of the Author, 12*s.*

Rose in Bloom. *See* ALCOTT.

Rose Library (The). Popular Literature of all countries. Each volume, 1*s.*; cloth, 2*s.* 6*d.* Many of the Volumes are Illustrated—

1. **Sea-Gull Rock.** By JULES SANDEAU. Illustrated.
2. **Little Women.** By LOUISA M. ALCOTT.
3. **Little Women Wedded.** Forming a Sequel to "Little Women."
4. **The House on Wheels.** By MADAME DE STOLZ. Illustrated.
5. **Little Men.** By LOUISA M. ALCOTT. Dble. vol., 2*s.*; cloth, 3*s.* 6*d.*

Rose Library (The), continued:—

6. **The Old-Fashioned Girl.** By LOUISA M. ALCOTT. Double vol., 2*s.*; cloth, 3*s.* 6*d.*
7. **The Mistress of the Manse.** By J. G. HOLLAND.
8. **Timothy Titcomb's Letters to Young People, Single and Married.**
9. **Undine, and the Two Captains.** By Baron DE LA MOTTE FOUQUÉ. A New Translation by F. E. BUNNETT. Illustrated.
10. **Draxy Miller's Dowry, and the Elder's Wife.** By SAXE HOLM.
11. **The Four Gold Pieces.** By Madame GOURAUD. Numerous Illustrations.
12. **Work.** A Story of Experience. First Portion. By LOUISA M. ALCOTT.
13. **Beginning Again.** Being a Continuation of "Work." By LOUISA M. ALCOTT.
14. **Picciola; or, the Prison Flower.** By X. B. SAINTINE. Numerous Graphic Illustrations.
15. **Robert's Holidays.** Illustrated.
16. **The Two Children of St. Domingo.** Numerous Illustrations.
17. **Aunt Jo's Scrap Bag.**
18. **Stowe (Mrs. H. B.) The Pearl of Orr's Island.**
19. —— **The Minister's Wooing.**
20. —— **Betty's Bright Idea.**
21. —— **The Ghost in the Mill.**
22. —— **Captain Kidd's Money.**
23. —— **We and our Neighbours.** Double vol., 2*s.*
24. —— **My Wife and I.** Double vol., 2*s.*; cloth, gilt, 3*s.* 6*d.*
25. **Hans Brinker; or, the Silver Skates.**
26. **Lowell's My Study Window.**
27. **Holmes (O. W.) The Guardian Angel.**
28. **Warner (C. D.) My Summer in a Garden.**
29. **Hitherto.** By the Author of "The Gayworthys." 2 vols., 1*s.* each.
30. **Helen's Babies.** By their Latest Victim.
31. **The Barton Experiment.** By the Author of "Helen's Babies."
32. **Dred.** By Mrs. BEECHER STOWE. Double vol., 2*s.* Cloth, gilt, 3*s.* 6*d.*
33. **Warner (C. D.) In the Wilderness.**
34. **Six to One.** A Seaside Story.

Russell (W. H., LL.D.) The Tour of the Prince of Wales in India, and his Visits to the Courts of Greece, Egypt, Spain, and Portugal. By W. H. RUSSELL, LL.D., who accompanied the Prince throughout his journey; fully Illustrated by SYDNEY P. HALL, M.A., the Prince's Private Artist, with his Royal Highness's special permission to use the Sketches made during the Tour. Super-royal 8vo, cloth extra, gilt edges, 52*s.* 6*d.*; Large Paper Edition, 84*s.*

SANCTA Christina: a Story of the First Century. By ELEANOR E. ORLEBAR. With a Preface by the Bishop of Winchester. Small post 8vo, cloth extra, 5*s.*

Schweinfurth (*Dr. G.*) *Heart of Africa.* Which see.

—— *Artes Africanæ.* Illustrations and Description of Productions of the Natural Arts of Central African Tribes. With 26 Lithographed Plates, imperial 4to, boards, 28*s.*

Scientific Memoirs: being Experimental Contributions to a Knowledge of Radiant Energy. By JOHN WILLIAM DRAPER, M.D., LL.D., Author of "A Treatise on Human Physiology," &c. With a fine Steel Engraved Portrait of the Author. Demy 8vo, cloth extra, 473 pages, 14*s.*

Sea-Gull Rock. By JULES SANDEAU, of the French Academy. Royal 16mo, with 79 Illustrations, cloth extra, gilt edges, 7*s.* 6*d.* Cheaper Edition, cloth gilt, 2*s.* 6*d.* *See also* Rose Library.

Seonee: Sporting in the Satpura Range of Central India, and in the Valley of the Nerbudda. By R. A. STERNDALE, F.R.G.S. 8vo, with numerous Illustrations, 21*s.*

Shakespeare (*The Boudoir*). Edited by HENRY CUNDELL. Carefully bracketted for reading aloud; freed from all objectionable matter, and altogether free from notes. Price 2*s.* 6*d.* each volume, cloth extra, gilt edges. Contents:—Vol I., Cymbeline—Merchant of Venice. Each play separately, paper cover, 1*s.* Vol. II., As You Like It—King Lear—Much Ado about Nothing. Vol. III., Romeo and Juliet—Twelfth Night—King John. The latter six plays separately, paper cover, 9*d.*

Shooting: its Appliances, Practice, and Purpose. By JAMES DALZIEL DOUGALL, F.S.A., F.Z.A. Author of "Scottish Field Sports," &c. Crown 8vo, cloth extra, 10*s.* 6*d.*

"The book is admirable in every way. . . . . We wish it every success."—*Globe.*

"A very complete treatise. . . . . Likely to take high rank as an authority on shooting"—*Daily News.*

Silent Hour (*The*). *See* Gentle Life Series.

Silver Pitchers. *See* ALCOTT.

Simon (*Jules*). *See* "Government of M. Thiers."

Six Hundred Robinson Crusoes; or, The Voyage of the Golden Fleece. A true Story for old and young. By GILBERT MORTIMER. Illustrated. Post 8vo, cloth extra, 5*s.*

Six to One. A Seaside Story. 16mo, boards, 1*s.*

Sketches from an Artist's Portfolio. By SYDNEY P. HALL. About 60 Fac-similes of his Sketches during Travels in various parts of Europe. Folio, cloth extra, 3*l.* 3*s.*

"A portfolio which any one might be glad to call their own."—*Times.*

Sleepy Sketches; or, How we Live, and How we Do Not Live. From Bombay. 1 vol., small post 8vo, cloth, 6*s.*

"Well-written and amusing sketches of Indian society."—*Morning Post.*

Smith (*G.*) *Assyrian Explorations and Discoveries.* By the late GEORGE SMITH. Illustrated by Photographs and Woodcuts. Demy 8vo, 6th Edition, 18*s.*

Smith (G.) The Chaldean Account of Genesis. Containing the Description of the Creation, the Fall of Man, the Deluge, the Tower of Babel, the Times of the Patriarchs, and Nimrod; Babylonian Fables, and Legends of the Gods; from the Cuneiform Inscriptions. By the late G. SMITH, of the Departmennt of Oriental Antiquities, British Museum. With many Illustrations. Demy 8vo, cloth extra, 5th Edition, 16*s*.

Snow-Shoes and Canoes; or, the Adventures of a Fur-Hunter in the Hudson's Bay Territory. By W. H. G. KINGSTON. 2nd Edition. With numerous Illustrations. Square crown 8vo, cloth extra, gilt, 7*s*. 6*d*.

South Australia: its History, Resources, and Productions. Edited by W. HARCUS, J.P., with 66 full-page Woodcut Illustrations from Photographs taken in the Colony, and 2 Maps. Demy 8vo, 21*s*.

Spain. Illustrated by GUSTAVE DORÉ. Text by the BARON CH. D'AVILLIER. Containing over 240 Wood Engravings by DORÉ, half of them being Full-page size. Imperial 4to, elaborately bound in cloth, extra gilt edges, 3*l*. 3*s*.

Stanley (H. M.) How I Found Livingstone. Crown 8vo, cloth extra, 7*s*. 6*d*.; large Paper Edition, 10*s*. 6*d*.

—— *"My Kalulu," Prince, King, and Slave.* A Story from Central Africa. Crown 8vo, about 430 pp., with numerous graphic Illustrations, after Original Designs by the Author. Cloth, 7*s*. 6*d*.

—— *Coomassie and Magdala.* A Story of Two British Campaigns in Africa. Demy 8vo, with Maps and Illustrations, 16*s*.

—— *Through the Dark Continent*, which see.

St. Nicholas for 1878. The First Number of the New Series commenced November 1st, 1877, and contains a New Story by LOUISA M. ALCOTT, entitled "Under the Lilacs." 1*s*. Monthly.

Story without an End. From the German of Carové, by the late Mrs. SARAH T. AUSTIN. Crown 4to, with 15 Exquisite Drawings by E. V. B., printed in Colours in Fac-simile of the original Water Colours; and numerous other Illustrations. New Edition, 7*s*. 6*d*.

—— square 4to, with Illustrations by HARVEY. 2*s*. 6*d*.

Stowe (Mrs. Beecher) Dred. Cheap Edition, boards, 2*s*. Cloth, gilt edges, 3*s*. 6*d*.

—— *Footsteps of the Master.* With Illustrations and red borders. Small post 8vo, cloth extra, 6*s*.

—— *Geography*, with 60 Illustrations. Square cloth, 4*s*. 6*d*.

—— *Little Foxes.* Cheap Edition, 1*s*.; Library Edition, 4*s*. 6*d*.

—— *Betty's Bright Idea.* 1*s*.

Stowe (*Mrs. Beecher*) *My Wife and I; or, Harry Henderson's* History. Small post 8vo, cloth extra, 6*s*.*

—— *Minister's Wooing*, 5*s*.; Copyright Series, 1*s*. 6*d*.; cl., 2*s*.*

—— *Old Town Folk.* 6*s*.: Cheap Edition, 2*s*. 6*d*.

—— *Old Town Fireside Stories.* Cloth extra, 3*s*. 6*d*.

—— *Our Folks at Poganuc.* 10*s*. 6*d*.

—— *We and our Neighbours.* 1 vol., small post 8vo, 6*s*. Sequel to "My Wife and I."*

—— *Pink and White Tyranny.* Small post 8vo, 3*s*. 6*d*.; Cheap Edition, 1*s*. 6*d*. and 2*s*.

—— *Queer Little People.* 1*s*.; cloth, 2*s*.

—— *Chimney Corner.* 1*s*.; cloth, 1*s*. 6*d*.

—— *The Pearl of Orr's Island.* Crown 8vo, 5*s*.*

—— *Little Pussey Willow.* Fcap., 2*s*.

—— *Woman in Sacred History.* Illustrated with 15 Chromolithographs and about 200 pages of Letterpress. Demy 4to, cloth extra, gilt edges, 25*s*.

Street Life in London. By J. THOMSON, F.R.G.S., and ADOLPHE SMITH. One volume, 4to, containing 40 Permanent Photographs of Scenes of London Street Life, with Descriptive Letterpress, 25*s*.

Student's French Examiner. By F. JULIEN, Author of "Petites Leçons de Conversation et de Grammaire." Square crown 8vo, cloth extra, 2*s*.

Studies from Nature. 24 Photographs, with Descriptive Letterpress. By STEVEN THOMPSON. Imperial 4to, 35*s*.

Sub-Tropical Rambles. *See* PIKE (N).

Sullivan (*A.M., M.P.*). *See* "New Ireland."

Summer Holiday in Scandinavia (*A*). By E. L. L. ARNOLD. Crown 8vo, cloth extra, 10*s*. 6*d*.

Sumner (*Hon. Charles*). *See* Life and Letters.

Surgeon's Handbook on the Treatment of Wounded in War. By Dr. FRIEDRICH ESMARCH, Professor of Surgery in the University of Kiel, and Surgeon-General to the Prussian Army. Translated by H. H. CLUTTON, B.A., Cantab, F.R.C.S. Numerous Coloured Plates and Illustrations, 8vo, strongly bound in flexible leather, 1*l*. 8*s*.

TAUCHNITZ'S English Editions of German Authors. Each volume, cloth flexible, 2*s*.; or sewed, 1*s*. 6*d*. (Catalogues post free on application.)

* *See also* Rose Library.

Tauchnitz (B.) German and English Dictionary. Paper, 1*s.* cloth, 1*s.* 6*d.*; roan, 2*s.*

—— *French and English.* Paper, 1*s.* 6*d.*; cloth, 2*s*; roan, 2*s.* 6*d.*

—— *Italian and English.* Paper, 1*s.* 6*d.*; cloth, 2*s.*; roan, 2*s.* 6*d.*

—— *Spanish and English.* Paper, 1*s.* 6*d.*; cloth, 2*s.*; roan, 2*s.* 6*d.*

—— *New Testament.* Cloth, 2*s.*; gilt, 2*s.* 6*d.*

The Telephone. An Account of the Phenomena of Electricity, Magnetism, and Sound, as Involved in its Action; with Directions for Making a Speaking Telephone. By Prof. A. E. DOLBEAR, Author of "The Art of Projecting," &c. Second Edition, with an Appendix Descriptive of Prof. BELL'S Present Instrument. 130 pp., with 19 Illustrations, 1*s.*

Tennyson's May Queen. Choicely Illustrated from designs by the Hon. Mrs. BOYLE. Crown 8vo (*See* Choice Series), 2*s.* 6*d.*

Textbook (A) of Harmony. For the Use of Schools and Students. By the late CHARLES EDWARD HORSLEY. Revised for the Press by WESTLEY RICHARDS and W. H. CALCOTT. Small post 8vo, cloth extra, 3*s.* 6*d.*

Thebes, and its Five Greater Temples. *See* ABNEY.

*Thomson (J.) The Straits of Malacca, Indo-China, and China; or, Ten Years' Travels, Adventures, and Residence Abroad. By J. THOMSON, F.R.G.S., Author of "Illustrations of China and its People." Upwards of 60 Woodcuts. Demy 8vo, cloth extra, 21*s.*

Thorne (E.) The Queen of the Colonies; or, Queensland as I saw it. 1 vol., with Map, 6*s.*

Through the Dark Continent: The Sources of the Nile; Around the Great Lakes, and down the Congo. By HENRY M. STANLEY. 2 vols., demy 8vo, containing 150 Full-page and other Illustrations, 2 Portraits of the Author, and 10 Maps, 42*s.* Sixth Thousand.

—— *Map to the above.* Size 34 by 56 inches, showing, on a large scale, Stanley's recent Great Discoveries in Central Africa. The First Map in which the Congo was ever correctly traced. Mounted, in case, 1*l.* 1*s.*

"One of the greatest geographical discoveries of the age."—*Spectator.*

"Mr. Stanley has penetrated the very heart of the mystery. . . . He has opened up a perfectly virgin region, never before, so far as known, visited by a white man."—*Times.*

To the Arctic Regions and Back in Six Weeks. By Captain A. W. M. CLARK KENNEDY (late of the Coldstream Guards). With Illustrations and Maps. 8vo, cloth, 15*s.*

Tour of the Prince of Wales in India. *See* RUSSELL.

Trollope (A.) Harry Heathcote of Gangoil. A Story of Bush Life in Australia. With Graphic Illustrations. Small post, cloth, 5*s.*

Turkistan. Notes of a Journey in the Russian Provinces of Central Asia and the Khanates of Bokhara and Kokand. By EUGENE SCHUYLER, Secretary to the American Legation, St. Petersburg. Numerous Illustrations. 2 vols, 8vo, cloth extra, 5th Edition, 2*l.* 2*s.*

Two Americas; being an Account of Sport and Travel, with Notes on Men and Manners in North and South America. By Sir ROSE PRICE, Bart. 1 vol., demy 8vo, with Illustrations, cloth extra, 2nd Edition, 18*s.*

Two Friends. By LUCIEN BIART, Author of "Adventures of a Young Naturalist," "My Rambles in the New World," &c. Small post 8vo, numerous Illustrations, 7*s.* 6*d.*

Two Supercargoes (The); or, Adventures in Savage Africa. By W. H. G. KINGSTON. Square imperial 16mo, cloth extra, 7*s.* 6*d.* Numerous Full-page Illustrations.

VANDENHOFF *(George, M.A.). See* "Art of Reading Aloud."

—— *Clerical Assistant.* Fcap., 3*s.* 6*d.*

—— *Ladies' Reader (The).* Fcap., 5*s.*

Verne's (Jules) Works. Translated from the French, with from 50 to 100 Illustrations. Each cloth extra, gilt edges—

Large post 8vo, price 10*s.* 6*d. each—*

1. **Fur Country.**
2. **Twenty Thousand Leagues under the Sea.**
3. **From the Earth to the Moon, and a Trip round It.**
4. **Michael Strogoff, the Courier of the Czar.**
5. **Hector Servadac.**
6. **Dick Sands, the Boy Captain.**

Imperial 16mo, price 7*s.* 6*d. each—*

1. **Five Weeks in a Balloon.**
2. **Adventures of Three Englishmen and Three Russians in South Africa.**
3. **Around the World in Eighty Days.**
4. **A Floating City, and the Blockade Runners.**
5. **Dr. Ox's Experiment, Master Zacharius, A Drama in the Air, A Winter amid the Ice, &c.**
6. **The Survivors of the "Chancellor."**
7. **Dropped from the Clouds.**
8. **Abandoned.**
9. **Secret of the Island.**
10. **The Child of the Cavern.**

(7–10:) **The Mysterious Island.** 3 vols., 22*s.* 6*d.* One volume, with some of the Illustrations, cloth, gilt edges, 10*s.* 6*d.*

Verne's (Jules) Works, continued:—

The following Cheaper Editions are issued with a few of the Illustrations, in paper wrapper, price 1s.; cloth gilt, 2s. each.

1. **Adventures of Three Englishmen and Three Russians in South Africa.**
2. **Five Weeks in a Balloon.**
3. **A Floating City.**
4. **The Blockade Runners.**
5. **From the Earth to the Moon.**
6. **Around the Moon.**
7. **Twenty Thousand Leagues under the Sea.** Vol. I.
8. ——— Vol. II. The two parts in one, cloth, gilt, 3*s.* 6*d.*
9. **Around the World in Eighty Days.**
10. **Dr. Ox's Experiment, and Master Zacharius.**
11. **Martin Paz, the Indian Patriot.**
12. **A Winter amid the Ice.**
13. **The Fur Country.** Vol. I.
14. ——— Vol. II. Both parts in one, cloth gilt, 3*s.* 6*d.*
15. **Survivors of the "Chancellor."** Vol. I.
16. ——— Vol. II. Both volumes in one, cloth, gilt edges, 3*s.* 6*d.*

Viardot (Louis). See "Painters of all Schools."

WALLER (Rev. C. H.) The Names on the Gates of Pearl, and other Studies. By the Rev. C. H. WALLER, M.A. Crown 8vo, cloth extra, 6*s.*

——— *A Grammar and Analytical Vocabulary of the Words in* the Greek Testament. Compiled from Brüder's Concordance. For the use of Divinity Students and Greek Testament Classes. By the Rev. C. H. WALLER, M.A., late Scholar of University College, Oxford, Tutor of the London College of Divinity, St. John's Hall, Highbury. Part I., The Grammar. Small post 8vo, cloth, 2*s.* 6*d.* Part II. The Vocabulary, 2*s.* 6*d.*

——— *Adoption and the Covenant.* Some Thoughts on Confirmation. Super-royal 16mo, cloth limp, 2*s.* 6*d.*

War in Bulgaria: a Narrative of Personal Experiences. By LIEUTENANT-GENERAL VALENTINE BAKER PASHA. Together with a Description and Plan of the Works constructed by him for the Defence of Constantinople. Also Maps and Plans of Battles. 2 vols., demy 8vo, cloth extra, 2*l.* 2*s.*

Warner (C. D.) My Summer in a Garden. Rose Library, 1*s.*

——— *Back-log Studies.* Boards, 1*s.* 6*d.*; cloth, 2*s.*

——— *In the Wilderness.* Rose Library, 1*s.*

——— *Mummies and Moslems.* 8vo, cloth, 12*s.*

Weaving. *See* "History and Principles."

Westropp (H. M.) A Manual of Precious Stones and Antique Gems. By HODDER M. WESTROPP, Author of "The Traveller's Art Companion," "Pre-Historic Phases," &c. Numerous Illustrations. Small post 8vo, cloth extra, 6*s*.

Whitney (Mrs. A. D. T.) The Gayworthys. Cloth, 3*s*. 6*d*.

—— *Faith Gartney.* Small post 8vo, 3*s*. 6*d*. Cheaper Editions, 1*s*. 6*d*. and 2*s*.

—— *Real Folks.* 12mo, crown, 3*s*. 6*d*.

—— *Hitherto.* Small post 8vo, 3*s*. 6*d*. and 2*s*. 6*d*.

—— *Sights and Insights.* 3 vols., crown 8vo, 31*s*. 6*d*.

—— *Summer in Leslie Goldthwaite's Life.* Cloth, 3*s*. 6*d*.

—— *The Other Girls.* Small post 8vo, cloth extra, 3*s*. 6*d*.

—— *We Girls.* Small post 8vo, 3*s*. 6*d*.; Cheap Edition, 1*s*. 6*d*. and 2*s*.

Wikoff (H.) The Four Civilizations of the World. An Historical Retrospect. Crown 8vo, cloth, 12*s*.

Wills, A Few Hints on Proving, without Professional Assistance. By a PROBATE COURT OFFICIAL. 5th Edition, revised with Forms of Wills, Residuary Accounts, &c. Fcap. 8vo, cloth limp, 1*s*.

Wilson (H. Schültz). *See* "Alpine Ascents and Adventures."

With Axe and Rifle on the Western Prairies. By W. H. G. KINGSTON. With numerous Illustrations, square crown 8vo, cloth extra, gilt, 7*s*. 6*d*.

Woolsey (C. D., LL.D.) Introduction to the Study of International Law; designed as an Aid in Teaching and in Historical Studies. Reprinted from the last American Edition, and at a much lower price. Crown 8vo, cloth extra, 8*s*. 6*d*.

Words of Wellington: Maxims and Opinions, Sentences and Reflections of the Great Duke, gathered from his Despatches, Letters, and Speeches (Bayard Series). 2*s* 6*d*.

World of Comets. By A. GUILLEMIN, Author of "The Heavens." Translated and edited by JAMES GLAISHER, F.R.S. 1 vol., super-royal 8vo, with numerous Woodcut Illustrations, and 3 Chromo-lithographs, cloth extra, 31*s*. 6*d*.

"The mass of information collected in the volume is immense, and the treatment of the subject is so purely popular, that none need be deterred from a perusal of it."—*British Quarterly Review.*

Wreck of the Grosvenor. By W. CLARK RUSSELL. 6*s*. Third and Cheaper Edition.

XENOPHON'S *Anabasis; or, Expedition of Cyrus.* A Literal Translation, chiefly from the Text of Dindorff, by GEORGE B. WHEELER. Books I to III. Crown 8vo, boards, 2*s.*

—— *Books I. to VII.* Boards, 3*s.* 6*d.*

YOUNG (*J. F.*) *Five Weeks in Greece.* Crown 8vo, 10*s.* 6*d.*

Published by

Facsimile Publisher
Ashok Vihar, Delhi-110052 (India)
Website: www.facsimilepublisher.com

Distributed by

Gyan Books Pvt. Ltd.
5, Ansari Road, Daryaganj, New Delhi-110002 (India)
E-mail: books@gyanbooks.com, Website: www.gyanbooks.com

2 222000 000332